GOD'S
INTEGRITY
and
THE
CROSS

GOD'S
INTEGRITY
and
THE
CROSS

Richard S. Taylor

FRANCIS ASBURY PRESS
of Evangel Publishing House

Nappanee, Indiana 46550

Toll-free orderline: (800) 253-9315
Internet Website: http:// www.evangelpublishing.com

Francis Asbury Press is an imprint of Evangel Publishing House.

ISBN: 0-916035-81-6
Library of Congress Catalog Card Number: 98-072660

Printed in the United States of America
9 0 1 2 3 EP 5 4 3 2 1

Contents

Foreword

For over half a century, Dr. Richard S. Taylor has exerted a profound influence on the Wesleyan branch of the Christian church. He has served the church ably as pastor, evangelist, educator, and author. He is the author of several widely-read books, among which are *A Right Conception of Sin*, *The Disciplined Life*, *Life in the Spirit*, and *Exploring Christian Holiness*, vol. 3.

Now comes the capstone of his literary works, a masterful treatment of the Atonement. Here is no glib appeal to a sugar-coated religion of sweetness and light. Here is no glossing over the appalling destructive power of sin. Here is no evasion of the judgmental wrath of God.

But here is the radiant assurance that the sacrifice of Christ on the cross represents the very foundation of personal and social redemption. Here is the inspiring hope of personal spiritual renewal. Here is the thrilling hope of a transformed culture and of a redeemed planet. And here is the grand fulfillment of "the abundant life." This book helps us to look beyond the flow of history to the time of eternal day.

I recommend this book without reservation.

Donald S. Metz
Olathe, Kansas

Preface

My life-long fascination with the question of Atonement was given an unpleasant impetus when for some years I was a reader of the senior comprehensive exams at a Wesleyan seminary. Year after year I was distressed by the cloudy grasp of this basic Christian dogma displayed by a very high percentage of the students. In trying to analyze this serious weakness, I found myself probing this wonderful but complex area of truth more carefully. Several times over the years I have attempted to lead seminars and teach courses on the Atonement at seminary level.

During most of that time I was a typical governmentalist—thumbs down on any kind of penal satisfaction notion! Along with many of my generation I had been shaped in my thinking not only by H. Orton Wiley but by John Miley. Through Miley's influence, in particular, I had come to assume that the governmental theory of the Atonement was more congenial to Wesleyan-Arminianism than any other theory.

However, the more I studied the Scripture the more restless I became about my too-easily-adopted assumptions. Very gradually I found myself convinced that Miley had missed the mark. This book is the result of my "conversion." And I have been delighted along the way to discover that as far as John Wesley himself is concerned, I am now more "Wesleyan" than ever before (See p. 114 f.). Therefore I am not the least apologetic!

Richard S. Taylor
Bremerton, Washington

Introduction

The cross of Christ not only demonstrated God's love but also revealed God's integrity. We are not likely to forget the first truth but in many quarters we are losing sight of the second.

There is a very close connection between our doctrine of God, our doctrine of the Atonement, and our doctrine of Scripture. The taint of liberalism at one point of the triangle affects the other two. Minimizing the wrath of God quite naturally leads to a moral influence theory of the Atonement, and both tendencies go hand in glove with a weakened doctrine of Scripture.

Many years ago P. T. Forsyth indicted vintage liberalism in the graphic words: "Any reaction of ours from a too exacting God which leaves us with but a kindly God, a patient and a pitiful God, is a reaction which sends us over the edge of the moral world."[1] Any adequate doctrine of God requires as its support an equally adequate doctrine of Scripture. Evangelicals have always regarded Scripture as authentically recording God's self-revelation and as accurately transcribing God's will. With some, however, the Old Testament is seen as a reflection of the cultural environment, resulting in a

---

[1]*Positive Preaching and Modern Mind* (New York: George H. Doran Co., n.d.), p. 354.

mistaken ascription to God of judgmental actions. But this is liberalism, not evangelicalism.[2]

The outcome of such dilution is not only an unbiblical view of God but a humanistic concept of the Atonement. Blood is an embarrassment, and the emphasis is to be muted. Such terms as "propitiation" are rejected, modified, or used apologetically. God does not demand blood sacrifices (it is said), least of all the blood of his Son.

Wesleyan-Arminians who see more in the cross than noble martyrdom or a demonstration of divine love, affirm some kind of a representative death as necessary to serve a sovereign governmental purpose, i.e., to be God's symbolic action in a show of public justice, so that forgiveness is not totally unlinked with the sanctions of law. This is often called the *via media* road, between Socinianism[3] and Calvinism.

But there has been a growing tendency to disparage any

---

[2]Walter C. Kaiser, Jr. points out that liberals have tended to invoke the principle of "progressive revelation" as a "rationale by which one can excuse and justify the more 'primitive' morality of the Bible by means of later revelation that allegedly corrects it." He answers this convincingly in his thorough essay "Legitimate Hermeneutics" in *A Guide to Contemporary Hermeneutics: Major Trends in Biblical Interpretation*, Donald K. McKim, ed. (Grand Rapids, MI: William B. Eerdmans, 1986), pp. 111-141. He says: "Progressive revelation, rightly understood, does not open the door to the the idea that inferior revelations were a prelude to more satisfactory and less embarassing later revelations" (p. 127). He refers to George Mendenhall's studies which reach the conclusion that "God's vengeance is no more than the exercise of responsible sovereignty" (p. 126).

[3]Socinianism is the name given to a theological school which developed in the 16th century out of the teachings of Faustus Socinus (1539-1604) and his uncle Laelius Faustus (1525-1562). They were Italian Catholics who denied the Trinity, fostered a revival of Arianism

idea of retributive justice imposed on either the sinner or a substitute. It is my conviction that such drifts are away from Scripture, and undercut the very foundations of biblical religion.

It is my purpose, not to minimize the relation of the cross to God's love, but to establish the relation of the cross to God's integrity. God keeps his word. The cross of Jesus Christ has PENALTY written all over it—penalty paid by One for the many. Those who have rejected the so-called Penal Satisfaction concept of the Atonement, and have rather opted for the Governmental Theory as being a sufficient explanation, have missed the depths.[4]

My thesis further is that the Bible teaches a penal satisfaction which is provisional and conditional. If this can be shown, the major objections to the penal understanding fall to the ground.

---

and became the fathers of Unitarianism and liberal Protestant theology. They espoused a very weak form of the moral influence theory of the Atonement, with Christ's death being viewed as the death of a noble martyr.

[4]John Miley (1813-1895), a Methodist theologian, is noted as the strongest advocate of the Governmental Theory since Grotius. However, Miley was strongly opposed by other Methodist theologians in his lifetime. T.O. Summers (1812-1882), a Southern Methodist theologian, insisted that Miley's one-sided position was not truly Wesleyan. He was supported by his annotator and editor, T.R. Tigert. Tigert asks: "Does Dr. Miley's theory adequately interpret Scripture in those profound texts which represent the demand for propitiation and reconciliation as arising among the divine attributes in the innermost recesses of the divine nature?" (Summers, *Systematic Theology*, vol. I, p. 272). He claims Watson and Pope as supporters for his and Summers' views, that "atonement is a real satisfaction to the demands of the divine nature, and that this is consistent with the true Arminian doctrine...."

Then, to complete the logic, it is necessary to show that the Atonement not only satisfies justice in a legal sense, but that it releases moral power for the believer. Because Christ died, the integrity of God may be accomplished in the believer. Sanctification is in the Atonement as well as justification.

The underlying hermeneutics of this book are very simple. First is the presupposition that the inspiration of the Bible extends to securing the accuracy of the narrative, whether in the New Testament or the Old. When the literary genre is obviously historical, and when it is clear that the writer expects to be believed because in his mind he is recounting sober history, we have no right to label the accounts myths, legends, or manipulated redactions. Especially crucial are the first three chapters of Genesis. Undeniably there are hermeneutical problems. But we need to see that the events of these three chapters set the direction for mankind, and thereby became the taproot of biblical theology and the foundation for the need of redemption. It is not too much to say that the entire Bible not only presupposes the basic historicity of these events but unfolds out of them. Scorn these chapters and biblical theology disintegrates.[5]

The second hermeneutical principle is that the New Testament doctrine of the Atonement is the interface of the Old, and that this conviction governed the thinking of the New Testament writers in every word they said about Christ and his sacrificial death. Christ's blood was the antitype not only of the Passover lamb, but of the blood shed on the altar in the

---

[5]In this too I am thoroughly "Wesleyan," as is demonstrated by Scott J. Jones' book, *John Wesley's Conception and Use of Scripture* (Nashville: Kinsgswood Books, 1995). See especially pp. 53-58.

tabernacle and later in the temple. Speaking of the Old Testament system, H. Orton Wiley says: "The sacrificial lamb became a symbol of the Lamb slain from the foundation of the world."[6]

---

[6]*Christian Theology,* vol. II (Kansas City, MO: Nazarene Publishing House, 1941), p. 221.

1

What Kind of Atonement?

Humanity cannot escape God. The race exists in an unavoidable relation to God, either of wrath and alienation, or of blessing and fellowship. Sin places us under the first; the Atonement makes it possible for us to regain the second. This is the essence of the Christian religion.

That Jesus of Nazareth was crucified under Pontius Pilate in 29 A.D. is a matter of historical record. That he rose from the grave the third day thereafter is equally established in the minds of Bible-believing Christians. Since this book is being written for such Christians, the historicity of these events is not at issue. Our concern is to understand, perhaps better than we have, the reason for Christ's death, and its meaning for us.

The Intellectual Challenge

There are always some sincere Christians who will ask, "Does it really matter?" Does our salvation hinge on a full understanding, or on our ability to nail down just the right theory? John Newton said, "Two things I know: I am a great sinner, and Jesus is a great Savior." Need we know more?

Millions of repentant sinners will be saved by the atoning work of Christ through the simple faith that Christ died for them. Their intellectual understanding of how this is brought about may be very slight and in this life remain so. With their last breath as redeemed persons they will cling to the Name and trust in an event which they cannot explain, but which excites them with wonder, love, and hope, and fills them with peace. Even the most learned are silenced in the presence of this profound mystery, and sing

> Amazing love! how can it be
> That Thou, my God, shouldst die for me!

But we must not conclude from this that a deeper understanding is not important, and should not be sought by all who have the intellectual capacity for it. And as J. Glenn Gould observes: "It is difficult to imagine one whose mind is so sluggish that he is content to drop the matter" with nothing but the information that Christ died and was raised.[1]

Two things should be said: First, while a full understanding is not essential for salvation, a false understanding may prevent salvation. There are heresies regarding the Atonement of sufficient gravity as to direct their adherents down not only blind alleys, but away from the Cross instead of to it. The result will be some form of satanic delusion which in the

---

[1] *The Precious Blood of Christ* (Kansas City, MO: Beacon Hill Press, 1959), p. 15.

end will lead to the horrible discovery of a misplaced and vain faith. How many pretensions and presumptions can be spawned by false notions of the Atonement! How many illusions of both salvation and security, deceptively lead into the bogs and marshes of antinomianism or legalism, and in the end forge more inexorably the shackles of sin! Surely it is clear that all of us as Christians should strive for a view of the Atonement sufficiently clear to enable us to detect distorted views.

The second comment needs to be directed to all who are called to be teachers and guides of others. If the theological beginners around us are to understand the Atonement—at least well enough to reach heaven—we who shepherd them need to understand it much more. The sheep may not know where the wolves are hiding, but the shepherd owes it to them to know. The patient may not understand the medicine, but the doctor has a moral obligation to understand it, and to be capable of giving instructions which lead to life instead of death.

The Futility of Human Answers

Very few serious thinkers in the world would deny that the human race is sick. The sickness is analyzed and probed and diagnosed daily in magazines, newspapers, and talk shows around the world. The human predicament baffles the brightest minds. People are doing things daily which they know they should not be doing, which augment life's confusion, disrupt homes and society, and add to the sum total of humanity's pain. What is the answer?

While the intellectual elite would never frame the question this way, in their hearts they know that at bottom it is a question of moral behavior. The honest way of phrasing it is: How can a sinner be separated from his sin? By denying sin's reality, says the humanist. By training and reconditioning, says the behaviorist. By altering the environment, says the sociologist. By better education, says the teacher. By better laws, says the legislator. By more money, says the politician. By improved health, says the physician. By self-understanding, says the psychiatrist. By the recovery of good culture, says the reformer. But all of these panaceas have a thousand times been weighed in the balances and found wanting. The ostrich-like denial of sin by the humanists prompted one of the world's greatest psychiatrists, Karl Menninger, to write a scathing rebuke in a book titled *Whatever Became of Sin?*[2] In it he sought to show that the concept of moral evil as fully accountable, blameworthy wrongness had to be retrieved from the wastebasket of discarded ideas and put at the heart of psychological therapy if any good was to be done.

Humanistic answers break down because they reflect an inadequate grasp of the problem. They never reach the profundity of God's holiness on the one hand, or the depth of sin on the other. The waves of sin's effects are cosmic. The endemic disease of sin is beyond the behaviorist's tinkering.

A morning spent in the Henry Ford Museum in Dearborn, Michigan, impressed me with the ingenuity of human

---

[2]Karl Menninger, M.D., *Whatever Became of Sin?* (New York: Hawthorn Books, Inc., 1973).

technology. In different sections of that sprawling display could be traced the development of steam power, electronics, and the automobile, plus dozens of other gadgets and machines designed to add something to the ease, pleasure, safety, or efficiency, of modern living. But not one machine in that vast museum was designed to turn a drunkard into a sober man, a libertine into a pure man, a greedy miser into a philanthropist—or a sinner into a saint. Henry Ford boasted that he would make cars available to every family, but he never promised that his cars would mend homes or always transport people to church.

Edison brought light—everywhere but to the heart. Men love darkness because their deeds are evil, Jesus said. They still do, even though surrounded by every convenience and comfort the human mind can contrive. Dr. Barnard pioneered the heart transplant, but when a young man in India wrote, "Please give me a new heart, one that is pure and kind and good," the great doctor was silent. Humanity's science and technology are utterly powerless to purify society and create good persons. Character is beyond the reach of the scalpel or test tube or drawing boards. It is equally beyond the reach of technology which keeps searching for ways to outwit the clever hacker, whose brains can show him how to crack the codes but not how to get the desire out of his heart.

Not only do science and education prove futile, but so also do the religions of the world, for they too are helpless in giving what the human person most needs: forgiveness of sins, moral power for change, meaningful existence, and assurance of eternal life. Neither Islam, Buddhism, nor Hinduism can offer these benefits as merciful gifts of the Most High God. They are religions of inexorable sowing and reaping, striving and struggling, rituals and rules; but all their religious exercises fall short of giving freedom from guilt, power for holiness, and inner fellowship with a holy Heavenly Father. Their ethical teachings and legalistic systems shatter on the rock of human perversity. They can show the path of virtue, but then cannot energize for its walk.

For an adequate source of moral power we must look to the cross of the Lord Jesus Christ.

2

Honing the Issues

A brief listing of the profound issues in any doctrine of the Atonement will plunge us at once into the intricacies of our inquiry. Is the salvation provided by the Cross for all or only a select number? If once received, is it forfeitable or nonforfeitable? Does the unsaved person have a responsibility in becoming a sharer in the great salvation? If so, what is the nature of that responsiblity?

Other questions, too, demand an answer. Did Jesus have to die for such a salvation to be made available? If so, why the necessity? Wherein is such a necessity grounded? Couldn't some other way have been found?

And what is the *modus operandi*? Is it an objective transaction of some sort between the Father and the Son which effectually accomplishes the salvation of all whom God intends to save? Or who elect themselves into the sphere of its power by a once for all act of faith? Or is it an objective satisfaction of some necessity in God which makes possible the salvation of all without arbitrarily determining the salvation of any? In contrast, is it a satisfaction not of God but of the requirements of public justice, a satisfaction demanded by the nature of that moral government which God has set over all personal beings?

And is it a salvation which to be fully consummated requires the voluntary and entirely free response of the sinners for whom it is provided?

These, and other such questions, cannot be silenced if we would seek to unravel the mystery of Christ's death, and avoid the bypaths and deadends of easy and superficial notions.

Some Points of Common Agreement

It is probably safe to say that among evangelicals the universal understanding is that Christ died to "save us." "Here is a trustworthy saying that deserves full acceptance: Christ Jesus came into the world to save sinners" (1 Tim. 1:15).

But what does it mean to be "saved," and how does the death of a bleeding, brutalized man on a Roman cross accomplish it? The answer to the first part of the question on which the largest number would agree is to say simply that Christ died to save us from hell. This is meaningful only on the assumption that the human race is in peril of hell. And indeed such is the case. Persons are estranged from God and under the sentence of eternal death because of their sins. "Your iniquities have separated you from your God; your sins have hidden his face from you so that he will not hear," explains Isaiah (59:2).

This leads to the second half of the question—how a helpless victim of crucifixion could have any bearing on this situation. The common understanding of Christendom is and always has been that in some way the saving virtue of Christ's death (1) sprang out of who Jesus Christ was, and (2) that his death was predetermined by God (Acts 2:23; 4:28) as a means of releasing us from the threat of eternal punishment and opening to us the option of eternal life in heaven.

This is about as much as we can affirm with the expectation of any widespread degree of unanimity. At this point all sorts of other questions begin to arise, prompting various answers and creating diverse (and often opposing) theological paths.

The Depth of the Need

We will never grasp the awesome magnitude of the Atonement unless we keep ever before us a single premise: The peril of eternal lostness is by far the most terrible fact of man's predicament. Nothing matters in this life in comparison with what happens beyond the grave. Our earthly life is but a flicker in the vast spread of eternity. Wisdom dictates that no hope could possibly be more relevant to human need than the hope of salvation from eternal separation from God. No amount of earthly success or human achievement could possibly outweigh the horror of this separation. If men and women have no transcendent hope, then life itself loses all meaning. Every sinner sits under a Damoclean sword, waiting only for death to sever the single hair by which it hangs.

But lostness is a horror experienced now as well as being an impending doom. It is a complex state of alienation in which we live. For our separation from God results not only from what we have done, but also from what we are. Our acts of sin separate us from God, but so does our predisposition to sin. Yesterday's sins may be forgiven, but if a sinful nature remains, yesterday's sins will be repeated. An Atonement which made possible forgiveness would be only half an answer if it did not also provide a cure for the disease. Is there "power in the blood" to change from sinfulness to holiness? Paul's anguished cry is echoed in our hearts: "What a wretched man I am! Who will rescue me from this body of death?" Can we also enter into his exultation as he answers: "Thanks be to God—through Jesus Christ our Lord!" (Rom. 7:24)?

A prime question therefore in any inquiry into the Atonement must be: Is it an answer to my inbred sin as well as to my personal guilt? Can Jesus save from a mean disposition? An evil heart? And does salvation include deliverance from the power of Satan and the fear of death?

The answer is yes. Therefore, when we explain the purpose of Christ's death, we must not stop with his "releasing us from the threat of eternal punishment," but must add, and "make us like himself" (cf. 2 Cor. 3:18).

The Word "Atonement"

The word most commonly used to designate what Christ did for us redemptively is "atonement." When we speak of it we often capitalize it, the Atonement. This can be said to be the generic term, for it has come to express the total Cross event in all its meaning. But in its very extension it has become ambiguous. The English word "atonement" is found only once in the King James Version of the New Testament, Romans 5:12. In the New International Version it is used in Romans 3:25; Hebrews 2:17; 1 John 4:30. Other instances of the Greek *katallage* are translated "reconciliation" (Rom. 11:15; 2 Cor. 5:18,19). Some would seize upon this as the clue to a full and proper understanding of atonement, and express the idea by breaking the word down into "at-one-ment." That is, reconciliation is the full and sufficient meaning of the word.

There are instances in the Old Testament when this seems to be the proper idea, as, for example, when Moses said to the people: "You have committed a great sin. But now I will go up to the LORD; perhaps I can make atonement for your sin" (Exod. 32:30). By this he meant: Perhaps I can turn away God's wrath and reconcile God to you. This Moses did, not by a blood sacrifice (as far as we know), but by representing the people in anguished and pleading intercession. God heard, and extended mercy, but not without punishing the people with a plague. Even here, prayer alone was inadequate to turn away the imposition of penalty. But the intervention of prayer negotiated a modified punishment—the plague instead of complete destruction. Thus a kind of reconciliation was brought about; i.e., an atonement was made.

But when the word "atonement" is intended to refer to Christ's death on the Cross, it cannot be defined simply as

"at-one-ment."[1] It is rather the Deed or action by which reconciliation becomes possible. In this Deed, the Three Persons
of the Triune God are involved. God the Father initiated the
Deed by the gift of his Son. The Son enacted the Deed as a
voluntary sacrifice of himself. Yet it was "through the eternal
Spirit" that he offered himself "unblemished to God" (Heb.
9:14). This same Spirit, the Holy Spirit, draws sinners to the
Cross, and enables them in faith to appropriate it for themselves, and offer it to God as their own. In this way the circle
is closed, and God and the sinner are reconciled.

To change the figure: the moral abyss is bridged, but only
in the sense that a bridge is put into place over which human
beings may pass. If we do not use the bridge, we and God
remain on opposite sides of the chasm.

Why an Atonement?

We need now, in an introductory degree, raise the basic
question: What is the ground of the Atonement's necessity?
There are at least six major explanations which have been
advanced:

1. The human race is in bondage to Satan and needs
   to be delivered. The ground of the Atonement's
   necessity lies therefore in Satan's claim on the
   human race, and the need to break his hold. This

---

[1]W.E. Vine comments that "the explanation of the English word as
being at-one-ment is entirely fanciful." *An Expository Dictionary of New
Testament Words* (Westwood, NJ: Fleming H. Revell Company,
one-volume edition, 1966), p. 86.

suggests what is known as the Ransom Theory, held by Origen and Augustine, to some extent by Luther, and called the classic theory by Gustaf Aulen in his definitive study, *Christus Victor*.[2]

2. The race is in debt to God's honor, and the debt needs to be cancelled by One whose own personal honor and deed are sufficient to counterbalance the dishonor done to God and discharge the debt of the repentant sinner. Hence the Atonement is not Satan-directed, but God-directed. This is the Anselmic theory, so named after Anselm, Archbishop of Canterbury (c. 1033-1109), and promulgated in his epochal little book, *Cur Deus Homo?* ("Why God-Man?"). This is perhaps the earliest systematic theory which could be called a Satisfaction Theory.[3]

3. Then there is the Moral Influence Theory, first advanced as a full-fledged position by Peter Abelard (1079-1142), a French scholastic. This theory says that we humans as sinners need to be drawn to God by a supreme demonstration of

---

[2]*Christus Victor*. Trans. by A.G. Herbert (New York: Macmillan Co., 1961).

[3]Anselm asks: "What greater mercy can be conceived than that God the Father should say to the sinner—condemned to eternal torment, and unable to redeem himself —'Receive my only Son, and offer Him for thyself,' while the Son Himself said—'Take me, and redeem thyself'?'" *Documents of the Christian Church*, Henry Bettenson, ed. (London: Oxford University Press, 1963), p. 139.

costly, sacrificial love; hence the ground of necessity for an atonement is totally in man, not in God. Abelard's belief was that love is the only divine attribute operative in providing redemption, and that the death of Christ served only to exhibit God's limitless and unconditional love. Abelard's teaching was the fountainhead of Socinianism (see Introduction, footnote 2), and the many subsequent moral influence theories, which have been the hallmark of theological liberalism in all its branches.

4. The Governmental Theory. This says that the human race is in a moral order which needs to be sustained by a demonstration of public justice, without which justification is not governmentally expedient. The Atonement therefore was designed to be "a deterrent to sin through an exhibition of its punishment."[4] This theory was first developed by Jacobus Arminius (1560-1609) and Hugo Grotius (1583-1645), a Dutch jurist, in reaction against both the hyper-Calvinistic doctrine of satisfaction and the loose notions of the Socinians.

5. A unique theory is advanced by Richard Swinburne, a twentieth century Oxford professor, which can be called the Ethical Theory.[5] Building his case

---

[4]Leslie D. Wilcox, ed. quoting Miley in *Profiles in Wesleyan Theology*, Vol. 2 (Salem, OH: Schmul Publishing Co. Inc., 1983), p, 93.

[5]*Responsiblity and Atonement* (Oxford: Clarendon Press,1989).

as a moral philosopher, he argues that the human conscience intuitively demands reparation for wrong doing, and that this becomes an inner urge in the sinner himself; i.e., a profound ethical instinct in the sinner is the knowledge that if he is to be made right with the person he has wronged—God, at the highest level—he must not only amend, but make amends. He must offer some form of atonement. Since human beings are unable to make sufficient amends for their sin to a holy God, God himself has provided the Atonement in Christ. This the sinner can offer by faith back to God as the ground of his release. Again the grounding of the Atonement is in man rather than God. But this is a much more profound position than Moral Influence. In that, the action is from God to man to woo allegiance. In Swinburne's theory, the action is from man to God to satisfy an inner need for atonement—an urge which God aids by providing his Son as a means to its satisfaction.

6. Christ's death is to be viewed as bearing a vicarious, substitutionary, and penal relation to the kind of death we as sinners deserve, of such a nature as to make our pardon morally justifiable. The race has offended God who is holy, and is therefore not only under his holy wrath, but is liable to eternal retribution. God's wrath needs to be propitiated by a substitutionary death which satisfies the claims of

penalty and removes the internal restraint in the divine nature from the free exercise of mercy. Broadly defined, this is the Satisfaction Theory.[6]

Rather than being mutually exclusive, these supposed bases for the Atonement's necessity to some extent overlap. Several can rightfully claim a degree of truth. But it is the conviction of this writer that the most profound and the most biblical is the sixth: The holiness (justice as well as love) of God is the ultimate ground for the necessity of an atonement. "Hold firmly to the nature of holy love," declares H. Orton Wiley, "and propitiation becomes the deepest fact of the atonement."[7] And R. Larry Shelton, while, by no means espousing the Calvinistic understanding of "penal satisfaction," pithily summarizes the truth by saying: "Through the sacrificial shedding of his own blood, Christ provides the means of propitiation and the ground upon which the case for acquittal and justification can be freely given to the believer."[8]

The Position Taken

This announced position needs to be expanded. The author desires to stand between extreme Calvinism and some articulations which claim to be Arminian. He desires to

---

[6]C.F. Wiley, *Christian Theology*, vol. II, p. 232.

[7]Ibid., p. 274.

[8]"Justification by Faith in the Pauline Corpus," in *An Inquiry into Biblical Soteriology* John E. Hartley and R. Larry Shelton, eds. (Anderson, IN: Warner Press, Inc., 1981), p. 120.

expose the fallacy of "finished salvation" on the one hand, and on the other the equal fallacy of rejecting a "penal satisfaction" concept of the Atonement.

The Calvinistic doctrine of penal satisfaction is generally understood to imply unconditional release for those for whom it is made, on the ground of "double jeopardy" (the same sin cannot be punished twice, once in Christ and later in hell). Arminians rightfully reject this narrowness, and believe that Christ died for all, and further, that his Atonement was provisional, not unconditional. Most Arminians also fault Calvinism on the ground that if Christ's death was an exact discharge of all debt, or the bearing of full punishment, true forgiveness becomes impossible, for you cannot forgive a sin or crime or debt for which full legal satisfaction has been made. The sinner or criminal or debtor is released as a matter of simple justice.

To escape this implication, some Arminians have swung to the other extreme and treated as anathema any theory at all which has in it the concept of penal satisfaction. Advanced in its place has been the Governmental Theory which sees the death of Christ an expedient of public justice, and in its nature a substitute for penalty.

In thus denying the penal or punishment nature of Christ's death, some Arminians have also shied away from an emphasis on the Atonement as a propitiation of the wrath of God, on the ground that God did not need propitiating. Only the interests of government required a public display of penal reaction; but a kind of penal reaction which served the office of penalty without being experientially penal.

This presupposes that the primary ground of the Atonement's necessity lay in the requirements of moral government and not in the divine nature. The attribute of love was the sufficient dynamic for reconciliation, and justice was involved only in its rectoral (public justice) relations. That is, there was nothing in God's nature or inclination which demanded atonement as retribution.[9]

As the chief exponent of the Governmental Theory, John Miley says, "There is no sufficient reason why sin must be punished solely on the ground of its demerit." Again, "All other ends apart, retributive justice may remit its penalty. It may do this without atonement."[10] The punishment of sin was not inherently necessary in the divine mind. God was free in harmony with his own nature to waive penalty and forgive in pure mercy. Apart from the interests of moral government, he could forgive solely on the ground of repentance.

The position of this book is that Christ by his death paid the penalty for your sins and mine, and that this was inherently necessary. The divine sanctions were not waived. Nothing is more biblical than the saying: "The wages of sin is death; either the sinner must die or a substitute must die." Christ died as our substitute, and his substitutionary death was directly related to the penalty we deserved. In dying,

---

[9]In his monumental work, *A Wesleyan-Holiness Theology* (Kansas City, MO: Beacon Hill Press, 1994), J. Kenneth Grider avoids impaling himself on the horns of this "either-or" dilemma. He sees that the Atonement's necessity is grounded both in the requirements of moral government and in the divine nature (p. 232f).

[10]*Atonement in Christ* (New York: Hunt & Eaton, 1879), p. 228.

Christ satisfied or propitiated that in God's holiness which demanded a penal response to sin, exactly as promised in the garden: "When you eat of it you will surely die" (Gen. 2:17).

The twin notions that in any kind of penal satisfaction theory true forgiveness is impossible, and that, because of the principle of double jeopardy all for whom Christ died must be saved unconditionally, are hobgoblins of constricted definitions. A biblical doctrine of penal satisfaction does not carry these implications.[11]

The rectoral or governmental principle in the Atonement is sound as a subordinate principle, but not as the primary principle. In attempting to avoid the unsavory implications of Calvinism as popularly taught and understood, Arminians are in danger of losing the true depths of the Atonement. In trying to get rid of the bees, we are cutting down the tree.

It is the conviction of this writer that Atonement serves the office of penalty to satisfy a necessity in the divine nature as well as a necessity of moral government. Jesus really took my sins upon himself, *but* in such a way that the release to me personally is subject to my response, and not automatic as a

---

[11]Wiley concurs with Dr. Tigert in his annotations in Thomas O. Summer's *Theology* that the satisfaction theory can be held apart from "its Calvinistic additions" (Wiley 2:258). Summers himself says, "It is not proper to think that the divine benevolence was ready to forgive sin without a propitiation, but the divine justice interposed a barrier.... There was doubtless 'wrath' in God to be 'appeased,' hence Christ is the propitiation for our sins. But there was no 'strife of mercy and justice'(Milton) to be *ended* by the atoning sacrifice of Christ. Mercy demanded satisfaction as much as justice" (*Theology*, p. 267).

purely objective accomplishment. It was therefore a provisional payment of penalty, not an unconditional discharge of all claims against me. Furthermore, the penalty was borne not for me only, but for all of humanity, and therefore all who hear have equal access to the virtue of Christ's redemptive action, and can by faith born of repentance make Christ's death their own.[12]

"Objective" and "Subjective"

To a great extent the discussion hinges on finding the biblical balance between the objective aspects of the Atonement and the subjective.

By "objective" is meant the nature of the Atonement as a transaction between the Father and the Son. This "objective" aspect of the Atonement may be viewed as closed or as open. If *closed*, the transaction is objective in the sense of accomplishing an absolute salvation, with all conditions in any way dependent on the sinner ruled out.[13] If *open*, the transaction accomplishes a kind of satisfaction to God's holiness as justice,

---

[12]In the interests of brevity and simplicity, the Racial Theory of Olin A. Curtis and Ethical Theory of A.H. Strong are not included in the above survey (cf. Wiley, *Christian Theology* 2:266-268). Both theories have much in common with the position being developed in this book. Also it should be noted that the Ethical Theory of Strong is not the same as Swinburne's theory, which in the survey above is also called Ethical.

[13]Jacques Ellul is representative of this position, but on the side of universalism (*What I Believe*, Eerdmans, 1989). On p. 192 he says, "Our free choice is ruled out in this regard. We are not free to decide and choose to be damned."

which makes the offer of personal salvation not only morally tenable, but which assures that the offer is truly an offer
only, not an arbitrary accomplishment. A. W. Tozer puts the
matter well: "Christ's work on Calvary made atonement for
every man, but it did not save any man."[14]

In the case of the objective transaction which is "closed,"
the sinners being saved may seem to respond freely; but they
are only discovering by the quickening of the Spirit that they
were "saved" back there when Christ died.

When the contrasting term "subjective" is used, the intended meaning is *not only* that the Atonement is designed to
make a real change in the "subject" (i.e., the sinner being
saved), but that the efficacy of the Atonement is determined
by the subject's response in allowing this power of redemption to have its fulfillment in her or him—a response made
not as an automaton, but as a free moral agent. This freedom
of the subject is such that he or she, through unbelief and
rebellion, can negate the value of Christ's death as a penal
death in his or her behalf.

Thus the Atonement in its nature is both objective and subjective. It is an event arranged by both the Father and the Son
which objectively clears the way in God's nature to extend
mercy, while at the same time maintaining public justice. It is
also an event which has personal and individual relations,
including the free offer of salvation to all who will repent
and believe, a salvation which includes not only justification

---

[14]*Paths to Power* (Camp Hill, PA: Christian Publications, n.d.), p. 16.

but sanctification, and which is available on thoroughly moral grounds.

By "moral grounds" is meant not only that the Atonement is a righteous ground for reconciliation, but that its benefits are offered to free moral agents, not imposed on automatons; and furthermore, that the offer requires the meeting of moral conditions. The fundamental moral condition is that we as sinners want to be saved from our sin sufficiently to turn from it. While such turning is impossible without divine aid (prevenient grace), it must still be our firm, individual decision.

The only action which can be called "moral" in nature, in distinction from that which is "amoral," is the free action of a free being in making choices in matters which she or he perceives and fully understands to be issues of right and wrong. Without requiring sinners to make a choice to turn from sin to God, the offer of salvation would be not even amoral, but immoral, for it would be the offer of escape from hell without requiring a turning from the sin which demands hell. This would be salvation without goodness; it would in fact be salvation while remaining willingly in a state and practice of badness. It would be a gift of eternal life which imposed no moral requirements. The Bible knows nothing of such a gift. As David F. Wells says: "Christ will only save us from sin, never in sin."[15]

---

[15]*Christianity Today*, vol. 35, no. 1 (January 14, 1991), p. 30.

3

The Cross Not an Option

Calvary was not an option. The cruel death of God's Son on a cross, if some other way to save the human race would have worked equally well, is not only inconceivable, but would be indefensible.

The Divine Dilemma

The assumption of the Bible is that any adequate and ultimate salvation must be from sin, the cause of humanity's predicament. It must be a salvation that lifts the load of sin's guilt and breaks the power of sin's grip. The sinner must be so changed that, not only is love for sin displaced by a hatred of sin, but also powerlessness toward sin is replaced by moral power to live without willful sinning. The sinner must cease being a sinner and become holy. Anything less is a salvation which falls short because the sickness remains unhealed.

But we have already seen that such a salvation is totally beyond the ingenuity of humanity. "Can the Ethiopian change his skin, or the leopard its spots? Neither can you do good who are accustomed to doing evil" (Jer.13:23). If men and women are to be saved, the initiative must come from God. The "good news" (gospel) of Christianity is that God has acted in Christ to make possible man's total deliverance from sin's hold. Its power, its blight, its penalty, its very tendency— all find their complete answer in the cross. Human wisdom proves utterly impotent. But Christ is God's wisdom, who becomes to us "righteousness, sanctification, and redemption" (1 Cor. 1:30).

It cannot be overstressed that the necessity of the Atonement lies in two realities: the holiness of God and the defilement of sin. Any ambiguity in our thinking at this point stems from our failure to grasp both the nature of holiness and the nature of sin. We have failed to see the total disparity, antagonism, and irreconcilability of the two.

The holiness of God makes it impossible for God to tolerate sin. Toleration would be surrender. God must do something about sin. God's holiness forbids neutrality or indifference. Holiness must make war on moral evil. It must be punished and it must be conquered. Condoned sin anywhere in the universe would unsettle the very throne of God.

The acuteness of the dilemma lies in the fact that the sin is in human beings whom God loves and is unwilling to destroy. Apart from this the conquest of sin by the divine holiness would be a very simple matter: just obliterate the sinner. Then things would be over and done with, and God could start anew with a new Adam in a new garden.

Divine love cannot accept such a solution, but seeks to save *this* race of sinners. The only possibility is finding a way of delivering the sinner from both the sin and its death sentence. And the deliverance must be threefold: from the penalty without waiving the penalty; from sin's power without coercion; from sin's alienation without loosening the moral terms on which reconciliation can be realized.

To say that God loves the sinner but hates the sin is to speak truly but not very helpfully. Sin is not a bit of fluff which can be brushed off as lint off a garment. It is not a wart that can be surgically removed and disposed of. It is not even a record of misdeeds that can be shredded and thus deleted from the files. Sin is the misdeed. Sin is in the sinner—his rebellion, love of evil, hardness, and depravity. It is not sin that needs pardon, but the sinner. The sinner must be punished if the sin is to be punished. For sin in the abstract cannot bear punishment. It is the sinner who is to blame. The guilt is his, not the sin's. The person who sins must bear full responsibility, *or else another bear it for him.*

And since the sickness is deeper than the deed, we would logically expect that God's answer would include not only pardon for the deed but cleansing for the nature. There must be a radical internal change. This is so fundamental that reiteration is in order. The sinner must be freed from sin's hold on him so profoundly and completely that his deepest affinities are no longer with evil but with holiness; so thoroughly that his love for God is the interface of God's love for him; so entirely that instead of being "at home" in hell, he will be at home in a holy, sin-free heaven.

If the sin problem, therefore, is to be solved, there must be provided more than forgiveness. Forgiveness deals with the removal of condemnation for sins committed. As marvelous as this is, it is not in essence a separating of the sinner from his sin. That consists of purifying the sinner from the sin itself, as a clinging pollution. The sinner is not separated from his sin until every sinful practice ceases, every sinful desire purged, every evil bent broken—all pride, unbelief, self-will, and every unholy affection; in short, until the person is made holy.

This is what John Wesley called Christian Perfection. "It is the circumcision of the heart from all filthiness, from all inward as well as outward pollution. It is the renewal of the heart in the whole image of God."[1]

And the cross is God's means for making such a salvation available to every member of the human race.

The Fulcrum of the Cross

Not the Incarnation alone, not Christ's example, not his teachings redeemed the race, but his death—this is the unanimous verdict of the New Testament.

While the Incarnation makes this kind of redemption possible, and the Resurrection validates it, the fulcrum is the cross. It was Christ's death that constituted atonement for sin. It was because Christ "made peace through his blood, shed on the cross" (Col. 1:20) that Paul could declare, "May I never boast except in the cross of our Lord Jesus Christ, through which the world has been crucified to me, and I to the world" (Gal. 6:14).

How could that be? Paul answers, "God made him who had

---

[1] *Works*, 11: 444.

no sin to be sin for us, so that in him we might become the righteousness of God" (2 Cor. 5:21). The writer to the Hebrews brackets his treatise by declaring that Christ "provided purification for sins" (1:3) and that he "suffered outside the city" that he might "make the people holy through his own blood" (13:12). And how precise is Peter: Christ "bore our sins in his own body on the tree" (1 Pet. 2:24); and Christ "died for sins once for all, the righteous for the unrighteous, to bring us to God" (3:18). Without doubt the Christian religion rests on the cross.

Humanistic philosophies and other religions pour scorn on the cross as a sign of weakness. It is to them an intellectual offense. But they miss the truth—this one difference distinguishes a religion of power from a religion of impotence. Paul put it this way: "But we preach Christ crucified: a stumblingblock to the Jews and foolishness to Gentiles, but to those whom God has called, ...Christ the power of God and the wisdom of God" (1 Cor. 2:23-24).

There was something in that death which overcame an otherwise insurmountable obstacle. "Sin is a problem," says James Denney, "and the burden of the book [Hebrews] is that God has dealt with the problem in a way answering to its magnitude."[2] There was in his death the satisfaction of some sort of holy and awesome necessity. We call that satisfaction the Atonement. In profoundly logical ways, the cross was God's means of reconciling the world to himself (2 Cor.

---

[2] *The Death of Christ: Its Place and Interpretation in the New Testament* (New York: Hodder & Stoughton, n.d.), p. 218.

5:18-9). It objectively accomplished the removal of a barrier to God's free forgiveness, and by so doing made possible our personal reconciliation to God. "Every other theory of God's mercy and love," says Walter Sundberg, "fails to reckon with the impassable obstacle of human sin."[3]

The fatal flaw in the definition of atonement as "at-one-ment" is its confusion of effect with dynamic. The Atonement makes "at-one-ment" possible and leads to it, but must not be dissolved into the notion that atonement consists merely in God offering reconciliation and our accepting it. If reconciliation were that simple, we would be completing the Atonement merely by deciding to accept God's offer.

If matters were thus, it would be hard to make any sense out of the cross. If the cross were not inherently necessary, if it were not morally indispensable to the mosaic of redemption, then revelation alone would suffice, and redemption would have come through Incarnation. Becoming Man, God the Son could have shown us how to live, and by the example of his life and natural death infuse us with moral courage. The Son who could say, "He that hath seen me hath seen the Father" (John 14:9), and whose teachings were validated by his miracles, could have proclaimed—without blood-shedding—the Father's offer of love and forgiveness on the bare terms of acceptance by the sinner.

In this case Gnosticism, which taught salvation through knowledge without such crude devices as blood sacrifices

---

[3]Walter Sundberg, "Discord over the Concordat," *The Anglican Digest*, vol. 33, no. 4 (Convention Issues, 1991), p. 35.

(echoed in modern Socinianism and its branches, such as Unity), would be proven correct after all. The only trouble with this benign scheme of things is that Paul does not trace our salvation to a revelation of God's benevolence, but instead to a transaction of the Father in the Son which was sealed with blood. Our justification, he says, hinges on having "faith in his (Christ's) blood" (Rom. 3:25). We. must see in that blood an atonement which even God's benevolence, as well as his holiness, demanded.

A Cross of Judgment

In what James Denney calls the *locus classicus* of Pauline passages on Christ's death, 2 Corinthians 5:11-21, Paul does not say, "Knowing therefore the love of the Lord we persuade men," but "Knowing therefore the terror of the Lord" (2 Cor. 5:11, KJV). Terror, because "we must all appear before the judgment seat of Christ, that each one may receive what is due him for the things done while in the body, whether good or bad" (2 Cor. 5:10, NIV). And the "bad things" stack the odds against us. Not lack of knowledge but lack of righteousness will damn us.

True, Paul himself is motivated by "Christ"'s love" which "compels" him. The same love which sent Christ to the cross is in Paul, and sends him to the world. But the urgency is derived from the gravity of the peril. Men are dead in trespasses and sins, alienated from God, and under condemnation. The "good news" therefore is that God has acted to transform Christ as Judge into Christ as Savior, but a transformation accomplished by his death, and not possible without his death. The remedy for our alienation and corruption lies not in the fact that Christ lived for all but that he "died for all" (v. 14). And that death was directly related to those very evil deeds of ours which would condemn us before Christ as Judge.

The Gospel is that "God was reconciling the world to himself in Christ, not counting men's sins against them" (v.19). But the reconciling was not accomplished by Christ as a *revelation* of God's love, disclosed on the cross, so that God could say, "See how much I love you! Now accept my love!" Rather, God was in Christ reconciling the world through Christ as a necessary discharge of justice—a discharge *in advance* of the future Great Judgment before Christ. He did on the cross whatever was necessary to make possible release from condemnation *then*. We know this because of Paul's only explanation, by which he sums up his discussion: "God made him who had no sin to be sin for us, so that in him we might become the righteousness of God" (v. 21).

The phrase "reconciling the world unto himself" does not mean what at first blush it seems to mean. The implied meaning is that in Christ, God reconciled himself to the world. Rather, the world was reconciled in the sense that barriers were removed and it was brought into a reconcilable relation to God. We know this to be the meaning because as a matter of experience, the world is not reconciled to God, but still is in rebellion against him. For this reason Paul soon is pleading, "We implore you on Christ's behalf: Be reconciled to God" (v. 20). There was nothing automatic about the personal experiential application of God's reconciling action in Christ.

The Atonement therefore is much more than a display of God's willingness to be reconciled; it is an objective transaction which makes "at-one-ment" morally possible. In the words of Denney, "Propitiation must be made for sin, if sinful men are to have fellowship with God at all."[4]

---

[4]A comparison of *hilasterion* in Hebrews 9:5, translated "atonement cover" ("mercy seat," NKJV) with the same word in Romans 3:25, translated "sacrifice of atonement" ("propitiation," NKJV), sheds light here, for in the Old Testament it is not simply God's mercy which makes at-one-ment possible, but the blood sprinkled on the mercy seat by the high priest which activated the mercy. It is this sprinkled blood which defines atonement. *Hilasmos* in 1 John 2:2 ("atoning sacrifice") and 4:10 ("atoning sacrifice") teaches exactly the same thing.

4

The Ground of
the Atonement's Necessity

Granted that the Atonement by means of the cross was an inherent necessity, the question naturally arises, What in the total reality of God, man, sin, and the cosmos was it which imposed the necessity? What was the ground of this necessity? Was the necessity grounded in the nature of man the sinner, or in the nature of God the Creator? Or both? The preliminary survey of these issues in chapter 2 needs expanding.

If we focus on man, we will tend to move in one of at least three directions. First, we may see the requirements of moral government as the crucial thing: the Governmental Theory. Second, we may see our need to be wooed as the central key: the Moral Influence Theory. Third, we may focus on the demand of the human conscience to make amends: the Ethical Principle. As was reviewed in chapter 2, there are other possibilities, but only these three will claim our attention in this chapter.

The Governmental Principle

The governmental motif sees God as the moral governor of all personal beings—not only human but angelic, both fallen and unfallen—and any other beings capable of being affected observers, whom we may know nothing about.[1] The interests of good government, in order to maintain God's control and retain universal confidence and respect in his character, demand that since all sin against God is not only private but public in nature (at least in its effects), God's action toward it needs to be public, as a demonstration of his wrath against it. Therefore it would be destructive of moral government, opening the gates to anarchy, if forgiveness were granted without a basis in public justice.

God's word set boundaries to the liberty of Adam and Eve and declared the sanction of death if these boundaries were breached. God's own integrity (which is to say, God's justice), is at stake in upholding this word. To say that God's word is at stake is to say God's honor is at stake. Honor is the

---

[1]Also called the Grotian Theory, after Hugo Grotius (1583-1645), a Dutch jurist and theologian. Following the direction pointed by his mentor, Jacobus Arminius (1560-1609), he developed the judicial view of the Atonement based on public law, which saw the death of Christ not as a vicarious punishment but a vicarious example, or representative death. Elements of the governmental approach are to be seen in British theologians Richard Watson (1781-1833) and William Burt Pope (1822-1903). However, the refinement of this position as a fully articulated and argued system was accomplished by John Miley (1813-1895), whose definitive statement *Atonement in Christ* first appeared in 1879, and his full two-volume systematic theology in 1892, 1894. Cf. vol. II, ch. VII.

praise, respect, and exaltation received from one's circle of personal observers. This is true of parents, pastors, govenors, kings, but even more true of God. God's promises therefore needed to be kept before the eyes of a watching universe to preserve his honor.

But what is more germane to the governmental motif is the need for humans and all created moral beings to be aware of God's wrath against sin, a kind of holy wrath which must act radically against sin. The relation of order to law must be seen by angels and men—or any other beings—as dependable in a dependable universe. Sinning with impunity destroys confidence and loosens the hold of authority, precipitating anarchy (cf. Eccles. 8:11). Personal beings everywhere must know that they are in a moral order and that a holy God is in charge. When rebellion occurs, as in the case of the angels and in the case of Adam, decisive and vigorous steps must be taken by God himself, to uphold his word, vindicate his holiness, display his wisdom, and reaffirm his inviolable sovereignty. There is no way to achieve these ends except by some form of public discharge of the claims of law. This means a public display of retribution. Anything less would unsettle the moral universe.

But in the case of the human race, God elected to satisfy the claims of law not by allowing the blow to fall on the guilty, but by providing a substitute who could and would take the blow (in a symbolic but acceptable mode) upon himself. Such a substitute would by his self-sacrifice uphold universal law, retain the respect of personal watchers, and maintain both God's integrity and his sovereignty, while at the same time making the offer of pardon morally appropriate—"so as to be just and the one who justifies those who have faith in Jesus" (Rom. 3:26).

The Governmental Theory does not say that the Atonement was necessary to render God merciful, for God is merciful by nature. The theory rather says that the Atonement was necessary to provide a moral basis for God to be merciful without violating his integrity as a moral governor.

Up to this point no fault can be found with the governmental motif as a reasonable ground for the Atonement's necessity. It is when this is affirmed as sufficient that many careful Bible students draw back.

Even more do many question the exposition of it by such thinkers as John Miley who stress that the sufferings of Christ were not penal in nature, but a substitute for penalty. The term "penal satisfaction" is vigorously rejected; yet John Miley concedes that the death of Christ fulfilled the office of penalty. But if so, the death of Christ was in *that* sense penal in nature, and in fulfilling the office of penalty constituted a *penal satisfaction*. This issue will be returned to later.

The Moral Influence Motif

If we turn to the second ground for atonement which is essentially anthropological, we come to a view which discounts any need for the public vindication of God's integrity, but insists rather that the sole impediment to full pardon and reconciliation lies in the stubborn hardness and intransigence of the human heart. The sufficient objective of any act of God called Atonement is to break this hardness down by a display of God's love as so magnanimous, so pathetic, and so astonishing that the worst of sinners will see God as willing to go to any lengths to persuade them to be reconciled. They will be encouraged to believe that God indeed loves them with an infinite love, and that if they but arise, they will find a loving Heavenly Father running to embrace them. This is the Moral Influence Theory.[2]

Unquestionably Scripture is clear that the Atonement is a demonstration of God's infinite love; for "God demonstrates his own love for us in this: While we were still sinners, Christ died for us" (Rom. 5:8). We humans at our worst are the object of God's love.

However, we are thrust back to the cold, hard fact that ungodliness is a choice. It is a stance of defiance and rebellion. Ungodliness rejects God, and lives in deep estrangement. Ungodliness is the character of those who do not "think it worthwhile to retain the knowledge of God" (Rom. 1:28). Not only do such persons deserve no mercy, they are not asking for mercy. *They ask only to be left alone.*

Angels must look down on human depravity and rampant wickedness in abhorrence, and find it unbelievable that God, so spurned, should deign to lift even a finger in humanity's behalf—to say nothing of rending heaven and his own Triune Being to come down among them, suffering their spitting and venom and the ignominy of a Roman cross in order to save

---

[2]First popularized by Peter Abelard (1079-1142), later adopted in one form or other by the Socinians, Schleiermacher, Bushnell, *et al.* A variation was the "vicarious repentance" of the New Theology. See Wiley, *Christian Theology,* vol. II, p. 264.

those who do not want to be saved. What incredible value God places on human beings, and how profound is his yearning to rescue them from their sin and from themselves!

The Moral Influence Theory, when standing alone, supposes that this demonstration of unbelievable love is within itself sufficient to awaken men and women to their corrupt state, arouse within them shame and self-loathing, and spark a desire for better things—a spark that would become a flame of hunger and searching, of confession and contrite repentance, of turning and transformation.

"Moral Influence" Blocked by Depravity

Can the sight of sacrificial love so affect a hard heart? When it seems to, is it not because there is already a hunger, even though dormant, for such love? These questions, of course, root themselves in the doctrines of humanity and of sin. If humanity is essentially good, even though misled by environment and browbeaten by appetites, and if humanity's degeneracy is only superficial (being "good at heart"), then for humans to be surprised by love might easily stir their latent goodness, and a response of love to love be the effect. The problem with this is that Jesus called the human species "evil" and the entire Bible, as well as human history, echoes the verdict. It was these evil beings who crucified Jesus and mocked him on the cross.

If—to shift our ground a bit—humanity is indeed fallen, but retains a measure of goodness, sufficient to have a substratum of affinity for God and holy things, then Satan's spoliation can be halted and his lies exposed by an unexpected and convincing revelation of God's love—sufficient to reawaken hope and strike again the sleeping chords of longing for better things. Obviously this presupposes liberal assumptions about humanity.

But if, on the other hand, the race is depraved at its core, (the position of both Wesleyanism and Calvinism), we must find some other way. Total depravity means that if left to itself, humanity would have no inclination to respond even to a dramatic show of love—indeed would have no more capacity to comprehend such love than demons have. If so, then quite clearly much more is needed than a show of compassion as a means of reversing the race's direction and of precipitating all the myriad flow of transforming influences called Redemption.

In the case of total depravity with its moral inability, any response to love would have to be created by direct regeneration, as the Calvinists have it, or else a capacity to respond created by prevenient grace, as the Arminians would say. In the Arminian understanding, a universal and unconditional benefit of the Atonement is the releasing of the first movement of healing into every human being, sufficient to create a bridge from deadness to life. As a consequence, Wesley taught, all persons come into the world under grace, sufficient to draw them to God and arouse longings for holiness.

But is there anything in the idea of moral influence to account for such a flow of awakening and enabling grace? Assuming total depravity, it is clear that a free response to God's love is only possible on the presupposition of this prior grace. And this prior grace is not an equivalent of the influence of demonstrated love; rather it is a measure of already-redemption which makes the dissolvings of hard-heartedness possible. It would appear that Christ's death solely as an intended means of wooing a lost race cannot be the whole story.

Two Scriptures come to mind at this point.

Paul's Commission to "Turn"

When Saul was converted, he was commissioned to "turn" men and women from "darkness to light, and from the power of Satan to God" (Acts 26:18). This was a staggering assignment. How could Saul—soon known as Paul—accomplish such a moral and spiritual feat? People then as now were caught in the viselike grip of their passions. Then as now they were motivated by greed, pride, ambition and lust. On what grounds would they be willing to turn from this darkness of their own willful, self-centered way to the light of purity and holiness? What would prompt them to renounce the works of Satan (even though they knew him not by name) and turn penitently and humbly to God? What would be Paul's power? His personality? Was human persuasiveness the catalyst? Or was it the story he told, of Jesus of Nazareth whom he identified as the Son of God, who became the Savior by dying on a cross and being raised from the dead?

That this *was* his announcement everywhere is without doubt. But did he present it as an exhibition of God's love, with an expectation that the mere telling of it would melt stony hearts and stir people to turn to this God of love—who was also a God of *holiness*?

The problem is, such an assumption is not supported by Paul's evangelistic methods. At Athens, for instance, he did not hold Jesus up as a show of love but as a means of deliverance from an awful peril. Paul preached the urgency of repentance, because God is going to "judge the world with justice by the man he has appointed. He has given proof of this to all men by raising him from the dead" (Acts 17:30-31). Paul did not shout, "Rejoice in God's unconditional love!" but "Repent!" The sermon was a warning of God's wrath, an appeal to conscience, and an exhortation to "turn" as the only way to escape the just judgment of a holy God on their sins.

Paul knew that divine love could have no power unless sinners first learned to fear God's wrath. The cross was held up as a revelation of our peril, an object lesson of sin, a pointer of doom. The ability of the sinner to see it also as God's appointed means of escape was dependent on their first seeing it as a finger of condemnation. "'Twas grace that taught my heart to fear," says the hymn, before it can properly say, "And grace my fears relieved."

The awareness of God's love in this divine act would indeed become overwhelming—but only for the penitent. Before the sight of Calvary as Hope must come the sight of Calvary as Wrath. Calvary must be seen primarily as God's means of delivery from sin and from hell, and only reflectively as an expression of love. So the impetus of any moral influence the heroic death may have is dependent on the prior perception of that death as a revelation of sin and its atonement.

When the New Testament is combed finely it becomes apparent that if Paul was to succeed in "turning" people, there must not only be the bare telling of the story, but the proclamation of the law and its sanctions, combined indispensably with the direct convicting and convincing action of the Holy Spirit, enabling hearers to come to their senses and awaken to reality. For that reason Paul declared to the Corinthians: "For I resolved to know nothing while I was with you except Jesus Christ and him crucified. My message and my preaching were not with wise and persuasive words, but with a demonstration of the Spirit's power, so that your faith might not rest on men's wisdom, but on God's power" (1 Cor. 2: 2, 4).

The influence of the cross is indeed moral, but not psychologically so, in the sense of an appeal of a noble ideal or exhibition of heroic sacrifice. Rather its influence is a Spirit-induced, supernatural influence, which itself is traceable to the cross, but requires a deeper explanation than the Moral Influence Theory provides.

Moral Influence and the Serpent

The other passage is Jesus' pregnant reference to the wilderness serpent as an explanation of the process of salvation. "Just as Moses lifted up the snake in the desert, so the Son of Man must be lifted up, that everyone who believes in him may have eternal life" (John 3:14-15). Then follows the classic declaration: "For God so loved the world that he gave his one and only Son, that whoever believes in him shall not perish but have eternal life" (v. 16).

The *giving* of the Son, Jesus makes clear, is illustrated by this strange event in the wilderness. God gave his Son to be pinioned on a cross as the serpent was fastened to a pole.

It is important that we get the picture here. Imagine hundreds of serpents crawling in and around the Israelites' tents, sinking poisonous fangs into fathers and mothers, children and infants, creating a horrible wave of suffering and dying. The serpent on the pole was the inescapable reminder of their sin and God's wrath. God sent the serpents—as the Israelites' very well knew—as punishment for their rebellious grumbling. Now they had to face their guilt and know exactly where they stood before a holy God prior to becoming recipients of God's mercy.

What that serpent was to their problem, so Jesus was and is to ours—not only a replica of the plague, and a means of healing related to their sin, *but a means dependent on seeing the righteous cause-and-effect relationship between the grumbling and the serpents.*

It is clear therefore that the God who in mercy provided the deliverance is the God who in wrath sent the plague. This fact must be included in our doctrine of God. The serpent then represented their sin and God's wrath—elevated before their eyes as a finger of shame. To look at it was to face the real problem and, in a sense, to acknowledge both their sin and God's justice. Jesus is saying that his death on the cross will be like that, yet more—the magnet drawing all that sin and all that wrath into himself, and by so doing becoming efficacious for our healing. An efficiency totally mysterious and suprarational (not irrational); an efficacy deriving its power solely from the decree of Almighty God.

On the natural plane, there could be nothing about the sight of a serpent on a pole which could neutralize the venom in the Israelites' veins and reverse the forces of death. If we are going to reach for a psychological rationale (which is what the idea of "moral influence" is), we would have to say that some symbol of love and hope, perhaps a flower, or a gold tiara, would have been more suitable on that pole—something to inspire faith and spark healing in those who gazed at it. But instead it was a *snake*—that which they most feared and hated, that which filled them with loathing and dread, that which was the cause of their pain. There could be no psychological benefit in that. No, the explanation must be found not on the psychological level but the theological. The moral implication is: if they were to be healed, they must first face their sin. This is always salvation's precondition.

Does this wilderness-serpent analogy, stated by Jesus himself, throw light on the Moral Influence Theory? Were the recalcitrant Israelites conquered by love? No, it was the snakes that brought them around. If demonstrated love had been sufficient, they would *never have been grumbling.*

Unless already drawn by prevenient grace, sinful beings do not necessarily respond to love, but frequently exploit it instead. People who are recipients of kindness feel they "have it coming,"that they "deserve it"; then they take it for granted and forget to be thankful. Who in all human history could have had more dramatic demonstration of divine love than the Israelites, who had been delivered out of Egyptian slavery, carried on "eagle's wings," fed supernaturally in the wilderness, and kept safe from every enemy? But sinfulness blunts the spiritual sensibility to all of this. No, love alone will not soften the hard heart, and turn people to God.

But pain will. The bitten Israelites did not look at the brazen snake in loving response to love, but because they were frightened, hurting, and dying. They were desperate and needed a deliverer. In such straits they were willing to turn to the God they had spurned, and humbly accept his provision for their deliverance. Afterward (hopefully) they saw this as an act of God's mercy, and loved him—or at least were grateful—in return. But it was pain that moved them to turn to God, not a show of God's love *per se*. Afterward, the more perceptive among them could grasp the insight that God's love was indeed acting, *both* in the biting serpents and in the brazen serpent.

True, "We love him because he first loved us" (1 John 4:19). God's initiating love is the source of Calvary, which means it is the source of the Spirit's wooing and convicting and drawing ministry and the source of every holy influence converging upon us, pushing us toward faith and responding love. But our love is not the inevitable and immediate response to God's love. It is only when we are thoroughly awakened to the awfulness of our sin, and when life caves in on us and we discover our helplessness that we are likely, in desperation, to look to God for mercy. Only then do we begin to realize the wonder of God's incredible love, and begin to love him in return.

The Ethical Principle

Before leaving the theories which ground the Atonement's necessity in man, some brief attention should be given to the Ethical Theory of Richard Swinburne. In his *Responsibility and Atonement*, he has an astute analysis of the psychology of the conscience. He delineates that aspect of our moral nature which creates within us an intuitive need to make amends for wrongdoing. This he believes is universal and imperious. Perhaps we can attempt to summarize Swinburne's view as it relates to the Atonement.

Swinburne shifts the ground of atonement from the necessity of penalty imposed by an external tribunal, to the intrinsic moral demands of interpersonal relations. The moral nature of humanity dictates profound ethical concern. Any wrongdoing or offense against other persons cannot be dismissed lightly, but demands a means of erasing the wrong with a view to the full reestablishment of the ruptured relation. Such a means of erasing the wrong must in the nature of the case come from the offender, in the form of repentance, apology, and some sort of reparation.

The necessity therefore is from our side rather than from God's side. God would be willing to forgive solely on the ground of repentance, as a simple act of mercy; but this would not meet the subjective moral demands within us as sinners. Our own sense of justice requires that there be reparation sufficient not only to satisfy the offended party, but our own conscience. Without such reparation we are not psychologically capable of accepting forgiveness and forgetting the matter. We cannot be comfortable until we believe the matter has as far as possible actually been righted; if it cannot be undone, then compensated for to a degree equal to the offense. To accept forgiveness without atonement would violate our innate sense of honor and justice. It. is our duty to make atonement. All Old Testament sacrifices express this subjective need to approach offended deity with an offering, as at least a token of reparation.

The theological bearing of this ethical need comes immediately into view. While atonement is possible for specific wrong deeds between persons, the matter assumes colossal and complicated proportions when the relationship is between a sinner and God. In simple terms, the sinner cannot make reparation or offer anything comparable, therefore must depend on others to help him. This help cannot be "others" at the human level, but can only be God, who in mercy sees man's predicament and by the gift of his Son makes a sacrifice available which the sinner can claim by faith as his own, and offer to God. In this way Swinburne keeps the cross central to the Christian faith, but posits its necessity in moral psychology rather than in the divine holiness. It cannot be confused with a works righteousness, because the efforts of the sinner are completely inadequate. God has provided the "work" of atonement through Jesus, yet Jesus makes it as a man, offering it to the Father in behalf of sinners as the perfect atonement which the sinner should be making but cannot. God is willing to accept it in lieu of the individual sinner's work of atonement when the sinner by faith brings himself under its merits, and in true penitence and faith offers it to God as his own.

The "bottom line" of Swinburne's theory is that atonement's necessity is grounded in man rather than in God. It differs from the Governmental motif by focusing not on the need for public vindication of God's honor as Moral Governor, but on the moral nature of man, which intuitively perceives the gravity of wrongdoing and the need to make amends. It differs from the Moral Influence motif by positing the necessity of atonement not in the sinner's need to be captured by overwhelming love, but by the sinner's need to be at peace with himself. God's love demonstrated cannot in itself create this peace in the sinner's heart. That is possible only when the conscience is satisfied that one has done what one can to make amends.

There is profound moral insight here. This understanding moves closer to the center than either governmental or moral influence motifs. But it breaks on the rock of human depravity, which has destroyed the normal functioning of conscience—or sense of decency—apart from prevenient grace. And it falls short of seeing in the cross a penal satisfaction for sin which deals with its demerit as it deserves, because such is an *inherent requirement of God's holiness*.

Insofar as the ground of the Atonement's necessity is to be found by looking at man, we have looked at three theories: (1) That man must see that he is under moral law, which a holy God will enforce; therefore an atonement is needed to demonstrate God's justice in upholding the force of law, as an exhibition of God's integrity as a Moral Ruler. (2) That man's moral condition is amenable to an overwhelming demonstration of divine love. Such a demonstration therefore is a necessity to win us, and to this end Christ permitted himself to be slain. (3) The need for atonement is rooted in our moral nature, and that Christ's action on the cross was God coming to our aid that we might have a suitable reparation to offer.

God the Ultimate Ground

Whatever truth there is in the anthropological grounding of the Atonement, it falls short of taking into full account the awesome holiness of God and the utter defilement of sin. It is in God's own holy being that the necessity for atonement must finally be grounded. Any ambiguity in our thinking at this point (as pointed out previously), stems from our failure to grasp both the nature of holiness and the nature of sin. We have failed to see the fatal disparity, antagonism, and irreconcilability of the two. God's essential nature requires justice; God cannot contradict himself. The humanity-oriented theories fail to pin down this fundamental fact as the ultimate ground. Therefore they must be rejected as adequate expositions of the Atonement made by Jesus Christ.

5

Death as Penalty

The philosophy voiced by some theologians is that there is no retributive punishment, only consequences, or remedial discipline (cf. chapter 6). Perhaps it will be helpful to reexamine the earliest circumstances of sin, then relate our findings to certain crucial passages in the New Testament.

Kinds of Death

When God told Adam and Eve that if they ate the forbidden fruit they would die, was God threatening a penalty or making a prophecy? That is, was God predicting what would happen naturally, or was God announcing what he would impose? Was death merely a consequence or also a divine retribution? And was God speaking of physical death only? Spiritual death only? Or both, but giving primacy to spiritual death as the ultimate disaster?

Let us begin our quest by observing that God created the human pair with a biological nature which was capable of death as a natural event.[1] This much humanity shared with other orders of being. The fact that God used the word "die" when he told them what would happen if they disobeyed suggests that the cycle of life and death, now seen everywhere in the natural order, was part of the original design at the sub-human level; therefore Adam and Eve knew what dying was. It is hardly likely that God would have delivered such a momentous ultimatum in terms totally foreign to the human pair's observation or conception. That they understood what God meant when he warned, "In the day you eat from it you

---

[1]Of course some Creationists vigorously deny this, believing that all death of living creatures (not including plant life) came as a result of the Fall and as part of the curse, and is included in what Paul means in Romans 8:18-23 by the subjection of the creation to "frustration," and the hope of its liberation from "its bondage to decay" (cf. James S. Stambaugh's *Impact* article, "Death Before Sin?" [El Cajon, CA: Institute for Creation Research, 1989]). While Adam Clarke does not believe the Romans passage has any bearing on this, he agrees with their basic tenet, that animal death is the consequence of human sin (*Commentary*, VI:105). This, however, is not a question which must be settled in this study, for we are focusing on the death of man in relation to the Atonement. It is hardly logical to say, as Stambaugh does, that to admit the naturalness of death at any level is to make a mockery of the death of Christ. The claim misses the radical qualitative difference between death in the animal kingdom and death as experienced by human beings and by Christ our Redeemer. Animals were not created in the divine image, destined for God's fellowship and eternal life, but were designed for an earthly, temporal life only. Therefore their death is irrelevant to the question of human death, and certainly irrelevant to a doctrine of Atonement. Death in the natural order may be normal, but death with humans is related to penalty and is a disastrous aberration. It is a tragic intrusion in human life, involving incalculable sorrow and suffering.

will surely die" (Gen. 2:17, NASB) is an implication hard to escape.

Apparently, however, physical death was not inevitable, for one of the trees in the garden which was permitted was the tree of life. When, after the Fall, Adam and Eve were deprived of access to this tree, it was expressly to prevent them from eating of it and by means of it "live forever" (Gen. 3:22b). Evidently the tree represented some divine plan of constant infusion of life which would counterbalance their biological capacity for death. But this perpetuation of physical life depended on their obedience. When they sinned they forfeited *the right* to any physical perpetuity they might otherwise have had. This banishment from the Garden was part of God's reaction to their sin. Obviously therefore, physical death was an imposed consequence and hence a punishment.[2]

The penal nature of physical death is implied also in God's pronouncement of the curse—primarily on the ground, necessitating hard labor if food was to be wrested from it, but also on the man's body, because now he would "return to the ground." As a physical organism he was "dust" and would return to "dust" (Gen. 3:19). Whatever plan God had to counteract man's nature as "dust" was now cancelled. Only the forthcoming plan of redemption, hinted in the Proto-

---

[2]For a quick survey of the positions taken by standard theologians respecting the question of essential or conditional immortality of the body—or of human life in this earthly form—see Wiley, *Christian Theology,* vol. II, p. 34f. Incidentally, the term "conditional immortality" has legitimate application to the body, but not to the personal spirit.

evangelium (Gen. 3:15), could reintroduce the prospect of physical immortality.

But of course physical death was not the only kind of death which occurred, or which God had in mind by saying they would "die." The wording of his warning suggests that physical death was secondary, and that spiritual death was primary. This is implied by the declaration that they would die "in the day" they ate of the forbidden fruit. While the processes of physical death began at once, it could scarcely be said that they died at that time. But instantly, upon disobeying, they died spiritually.

Spiritual death, we learn from the Scripture elsewhere, has an immediate stage and an ultimate, final stage.[3] The immediate stage is guilt, alienation, and depravity (or the loss of spiritual life) while the ultimate stage the Bible calls "the second death" (Rev. 2:11; 20:6,14; 21:8). This is final, eternal, and irreversible.

A very important distinction needs to be made here. The immediate spiritual death which occurred was a natural consequence of disobedience, not precisely a retribution or penalty. However, because guilt and depravity are self-induced, the sinner lives under the threat of sin's ultimate penalty: eternal separation from God. It is this peril which constitutes humanity's deepest jeopardy, and which imposes the deepest need for Atonement. Therefore the penal nature of

---

[3]For further discussion of the biblical teaching on death, see the "The New Birth," in *Projecting Our Heritage*, comp. by Myron F. Boyd and Merne A. Harris (Kansas City, MO: Beacon Hill Press, 1969), p. 57f.

the atonement of necessity answers to the penal nature of the Second Death.

The Garden Event

It may aid us in perceiving the gravity of humanity's condition if we trace the unfolding of spiritual death as it was experienced by Adam and Eve, and has been experienced by every member of the race since. Let us trace these components.

First, there would be a sense of guilt—a painful consciousness of having done wrong; consequent to this would be fear and alienation, possibly shame. This profoundly traumatic wrenching of the entire being prompted hiding.

The consequence would be objective as well as subjective, consisting of a break with God. By its very nature, the disobedience would constitute such a break, for their sin would be a rejection of God—his law and his authority. It would be a repudiation of their place in the divine scheme of things, as stewards acting for God under his jurisdiction and within the restraints of a theocratic order. They would be asserting independence from this order; in effect, setting up a rival kingdom. Here then is an assertion of self in defiance of God's sovereignty. Obviously this constitutes a rupture.

Such a rupture would include severance between the human spirit and the Holy Spirit. Since the Holy Spirit had not been permitted to rule, he could not remain within, but must assume a position outside of man as an agent incognito.

The domino effect of this would be a radical dislocation of man's moral and spiritual nature. Since self had assumed the throne, all the forces of personality, interrelationships, and human life in general would become perverted toward self-idolatry. As a datum of biblical history, this is exactly what happened, with devastating effects in every generation since.

But self-idolatry blinds to one's true self-interest, blunts the moral sense, and creates progressive and cumulative proclivities toward evil and obtuseness toward good. This is necessarily true because the perspective from which persons now view life is no longer a true perspective, but rather is askew. Bereft of the inner strength and wisdom derived from the Spirit, one cannot avoid the deterioration of the entire person. Depravity, then, is an inevitable consequence of disobedience.

Obviously the primary tragedy of the Fall was not physical death, but spiritual death, a kind of death which flowed inevitably from the rebellion. *This was not penal in itself, but was of such a nature that it deserved and morally required penalty.* This is true because the depravity was bound up with the disobedience as a cause/effect moral unity. And since the human pair were to blame for the disobedience, they were equally to blame for the depravity which resulted.

God's Reactions

The most obvious and inherently logical effect of the human pair's sin on God would be displeasure. For God to be so morally indifferent that he would not mind their disobedience would leave no rational ground for setting up a divine rule in the first place. If the prohibition respecting the tree of the knowledge of good and evil was authentically God's will, then despising the prohibition must of necessity be contrary to God's will. If contrary, any predication of moral nature in God at all would argue for a reaction of radical displeasure.

Furthermore, it is equally unthinkable that divine displeasure would prompt no divine action. The doctrine of immutability certainly does not imply moral passivity.

We may presume therefore that God's reaction would be one of displeasure, and that his displeasure would be expressed in some form of action. As a matter of fact, of course, it was. It was first expressed as a curse pronounced on the serpent. Then to the woman God said,

> I will greatly increase your pains in
>   childbearing;
> with pain you will give birth to children.
> Your desire will be for your husband,
> and he will rule over you (Gen. 3:16).

To the man he said,

> Because you listened to your wife and ate from
> the tree about which I commanded you, 'You
> must not eat of it,'
> Cursed is the ground because of you;
> through painful toil you will eat of it
>   all the days of your life
> It will produce thorns and thistles for you,
>   and you will eat the plants of the field.
> By the sweat of your brow you will eat your
>   food
> until you return to the ground,
>   since from it you were taken;
> for dust you are
>   and to dust you will return.

In addition to these pronouncements, God banished the pair from the garden (as has already been mentioned) to prevent their partaking of the tree of life and thus perpetuating their life on earth.

However we have now quietly moved away from the category of natural consequences. Human disease, depravity, and death can be accounted for as inherent results of sin, without the necessity of God's punitive intervention. But now we are talking about something else: the personal reaction of God himself. It would be straining to call this a "natural" consequence, since it is a personal intervention, as an interaction between persons, on the part of God.

It is possible to construe these divine statements and actions as disciplinary as well as punitive. In this case the "judgments" may be thought of as divinely initiated steps toward restoration, rather than as punishments *per se*. At once, however, the question arises concerning the serpent. In what sense could the curse on it be disciplinary? The natural sense of the language suggests that God was imposing punishment on the serpent, for as far as the Bible indicates, reclamation of the evil power which the serpent symbolizes is not in God's redemptive program. The idea of discipline toward rehabilitation therefore would be meaningless. That the curse on the serpent was a consequence is clear from God's words, "Because you have done this," … but the prostration of the serpent to the ground as a crawling thing was a supernatural imposition; it certainly could not be called a "natural" consequence. Therefore it, at least, was punitive in nature.

Can the language used by God in his pronouncements to Adam and Eve be limited to a disciplinary sense? Admittedly, even then God was thinking of their redemption. This is indicated by what has come to be called the Protoevangelium:

> And I will put enmity
> between you and the woman,
> and between your offspring and hers;
> he will crush your head,
> and you will strike his heel (3:15).

Since their redemption was God's ultimate purpose, this would logically affect the purpose of the curses. The imposition of pain must have been seen by God as a necessary means of humbling man, fostering within him a sense of dependence, and thus creating a psychology of fears and needs which would tend to push man back toward God. Such would be the disciplinary purpose.

But we must not minimize the element here of punishment. These divine actions were not "natural" effects, and were more than disciplinary; they were also imposed sentences by an offended Sovereign, who was reacting to deliberate sin in a manner dictated by the divine holiness.

That God's pronouncements were punitive is supported by the use of the word "curse" (Heb., *arar*). Examination of the use of this word in the Old Testament reveals clearly that it carries a meaning of pain or rejection imposed as an expression of God's wrath. When God said to Cain, "Now you are under a curse," God was clearly pronouncing a penalty for the sin of killing Abel.

Clearly, the dynamics of the Garden debacle are radically different if God's threat of death was a pronouncement of penalty as well as a prediction of natural consequences. The concept of penalty has within it the implication that disobedience deserves punishment, and that the specific punishment which the sinner deserves is death. Further, the concept has within it the note of necessity: that the imposition of penalty is a moral necessity, apart from any consideration of rehabilitation; and that treating it as an option would be a breach of the divine holiness. From this standpoint we must say that death was imposed not primarily as a disciplinary measure in order to recover, but because justice demands that wrongs be avenged. But even more germane—God had pronounced a sentence in advance, and justice required that God carry it out. Let us keep the integrity of God always before us.

What do we have then? Human depravity in itself is not imposed by God as a punishment. It can be accounted for in terms of natural consequence. The alienation from God is the consequence of both the act of sin and the depravity. This is in a sense a "natural" moral consequence, in view of the antithetical nature of sin and holiness. But the judicial imposition of pain in this life and threat of eternal separation from God—assumed throughout the Bible—is consequence under divine wrath. Both natural consequence and moral consequence merge into punishments. This is essential to the personal level of the action. God, a holy Person, is dealing with persons whom he has made sufficiently like himself to be thoroughly responsible, therefore properly subject to punitive action.

Paul's Verdict on Death

That human death is the consequence of sin is declared by Paul: "... sin entered the world through one man, and death through sin" (Rom. 5:12). That it is a *penal* consequence is made clear in the balance of the paragraph, as can be seen in the following statements: "The judgment followed one sin and brought condemnation" (v. 16b); "For if, by the trespass of one man, death reigned through that one man..." (v.17). While physical death is included, the point of Paul's attention is spiritual death. The entire passage, including the transition into chapter 6, is a contrast between the spiritual death suffering from and in Adam and the spiritual life enjoyed in and through Christ. While physical death is in the background, it is not the focal issue.[4]

Spiritual life in Christ out of spiritual death leads Paul's argument in chapter 6. Our bodies are to be consecrated to God and used in his service, as is appropriate for those who "have been brought from death [spiritual] to life [spiritual]" (v. 13). Obedience to sin as slaves will lead "to death" (spiritual, v. 16). If we permit the grace of God to set us free from sin and make us "slaves to God," the benefit we reap "leads to holiness, and the result is eternal life" (v. 22). "For the wages of sin is death [spiritual], but the gift of God is eternal life in Christ Jesus our Lord" (v. 23).

---

[4]Wiley's word is helpful here: "Hereditary depravity, then, is only the law of natural heredity, but that law operating under the penal consequences of Adam's sin" (*Christian Theology*, vol. II, p. 125). He also calls attention to the fact that both "Mr. Watson and Mr. Howe argue the penal nature of depravity from the retraction of the Spirit" (p. 127).

The distinction between physical death and spiritual death is made still clearer in chapters 7-8. The "death" which is conjoined with "sin" as "the law of sin and death" (8:2) is spiritual death. The "mind of sinful man is death"—this also is spiritual death. The distinction is spelled out in v. 10: "But if Christ is in you, your body is dead because of sin, yet your spirit is alive because of righteousness." Physical death is the result of sin, but Christ did not die to exempt us from it. Christians will die as well as sinners. Obviously, therefore, physical death is not the acute problem or the primary concern of the Atonement. Christ died to atone for our sin, and deliver us, in this life, from it. The Atonement does not aim merely at the effects of sin, but primarily at the cause of the effects.

Following the Great Deliverance (from sin) will come the secondary deliverance, saving us out of physical death. The Spirit that raised Jesus "will also give life to your mortal bodies" (v. 11). This is not a reference to divine healing now—though of course at times the Spirit does that too. It is a reference to the time when the possibility of bodily perpetuity which Adam and Eve forfeited in the Garden will be given back to us—"when the perishable must clothe itself with the imperishable, and the mortal with immortality," and death will be "swallowed up in victory" (1 Cor. 15:54). Therefore, while physical death is a calamity and Christ died to remedy it, that is both secondary and deferred. For now the important thing is holiness and its maintenance. Physical death is not addressed in v. 13, "For if you live according to the sinful nature you will die," *for that will be our experience in any case,* but rather spiritual death. It is a warning against the notion that careless living after the new birth will not cost us our eternal life!

Death and Justice

In expounding justification by faith rather than by works, Paul declares a basic moral principle: "Now to the one who works, his wage is not reckoned as a favor, but as what is due" (Rom. 4:4, NASB). Eternal life can never be seen as a free gift if it is earned by works, but as simple justice. The "works" would have to be not just good deeds, but total sinlessnes— from accountability on. Because of original sin, this is a practical impossibility, as Paul makes clear in Romans 1–3. Therefore eternal life, if to be experienced at all, must be made available by some others means. This God has done in Christ.

But how Christ's death is related to the basic moral principle of justice vs. favor (or "wages" vs. "gift") is suggested by the verse we just noted above: "For the wages of sin is death, but the free gift of God is eternal life in Christ Jesus our Lord" (6:23, NASB). While "wage" in 4:4 is *misthos* and "wages" in 6:23 is the plural of *opsonion*, the meaning is the same. In both cases Paul speaks of a wage as that which has been earned, and is therefore payable as a matter of justice. Payment is obligatory. But if eternal life is an award due those who (hypothetically) earn it, the death which is the wages of sin is equally "due"; and to be honorable, wages must be paid. God in his holiness, therefore, cannot withhold from the sinner what he has earned, and in its place substitute eternal life in Jesus Christ, unless the "in Christ" means that the death due the sinner has been suffered by Christ. The moral principle of obligation is not cavalierly ignored; it is fully satisfied. Justice remains intact. But the payment of sin's wages to Christ as our substitute obviates the necessity of paying it to us. Eternal life, then, can be said to be a "free gift" only in the sense that it costs us nothing. For God and Father and God the Son, our eternal life is not free, but costly indeed.

Bearing Our Curse

The penal nature of death and the penal nature of Christ's substitutionary death for us is nowhere more graphically and incontrovertibly set forth than in Paul's discussion of Christ "becoming a curse for us" (Gal. 3:13; cf. 10-14). Paul states: "Christ redeemed us from the curse of the law by becoming a curse for us, for it is written: 'Cursed is everyone who is hung on a tree.'"[5] The "curse of the law" is not the law itself—as if the human race was cursed simply by having been given the law—but rather the curse pronounced on those who do "not continue in all things which are written in the book of the law, to do them" (v. 10; cf. Deut. 27:26). The law allows no exceptions or leeway. A curse rests on the violator for every infrac-

---

[5]That the apostles considered this form of expression significant for a proper understanding of the nature of Christ's death is indicated by Acts 5:30; 10:39; 13:29.

W. E. Vine comments on Gal. 6:13: "it is used concretely of Christ, as having 'become a curse' for us, i.e., by voluntarily undergoing on the Cross the appointed penalty of the curse. He was thus identified, on our behalf, with the doom of sin." *An Expository Dictionary of New Testament Words*, vol. 1 (Westwood, NJ: Fleming H. Revell Company, 1966), p. 262.

tion, just as the curse settled upon Adam and Eve for their one infraction, and upon Cain for his one murder. The curse is the official pronouncement of God's displeasure and his stance of moral opposition to that person (cf. Ps.34:16, *et al.*). As we have already seen, to be under a divine curse is to be under the wrath of God.

Christ redeems us in the sense that he delivers us from the curse and condemnation of violated law, thereby reconciling us to God. This he does by becoming "a curse for us" (*huper*, in our behalf). The particular curse borne by Jesus was the curse pronounced on "everyone who is hung on a tree" (v. 13b, from Deut. 21:22-23). The Deuteronomic passage determines the nature of this curse beyond doubt. "If a man has committed a sin deserving of death" and is hanged for it, he bears the curse of God, "for he who is hanged is accursed of God." The hanging does not *bring* the curse, it *symbolizes* the curse by bearing witness to the victim's guilt. He is cursed because of the crime he has committed, to which the hanging is testimony and for which it is punishment.

Since sin in the sense of *parabasis* always deserves death, all willful sinners are under the curse, even though not yet hung "on a tree." Christ's hanging *in our behalf* can only be a substitutional hanging, which makes possible our release from personally bearing the sentence. This must be true, since Jesus could not be under a curse for his own sin. To become a "curse for us" is meaningful only if Jesus bore our curse *in our stead* by permitting himself to be hung on the tree which rightfully should have borne us. This is death which is completely and sufficiently vicarious, and at the same time thoroughly penal.

Yet we are not compelled to say that Jesus was being punished. He did not become guilty of our sins. That would be impossible, because he did not do them. But Jesus bore in our stead the curse of God's wrath as if the sins were his own. His cry of dereliction could imply nothing less. *This* was the cup which he drank, not the mere fact of dying. He suffered not only with malefactors, but *as* a malefactor, yet without being one. All the wrath of a holy God against every sin from Adam's to the last disobedience in time Jesus drew into himself. But it was because of and on behalf of *our* sin, not his own. On the cross Christ became humanity's lightning rod, catching and absorbing (not deflecting) the bolts of divine wrath deserved by us.

How movingly clear is John R. W. Stott's way of putting it: "The sinless one was 'made sin for us', which must mean that he bore the penalty of our sin instead of us, and redeemed us from the law's curse by 'becoming a curse for us', which must mean that the curse of the law lying upon us for our disobedience was transferred to him, so that he bore it instead of us."[6]

Yet God put him there. Jesus was a willing substitute (in spite of the anguish); but it was the substitution of obedience to a God who in his holy perfections saw the sacrifice, not as one option, but as the inescapable necessity.

---

[6]*The Cross of Christ* (Downers Grove, IL: InterVarsity Press, 1986), p. 148.

Significance for Atonement

The primary significance of this chapter for a doctrine of atonement is twofold: First, for Christ's death to be a full substitute for us, his death must be related to spiritual death as well as physical death. If substitution in physical death could have been sufficient for the making of atonement, Jesus could just as well have died in his bed of old age. Second, his death must be penal in nature. He died an adjuticatory death, certainly by man, and in a profound sense by God also. Great stress in the New Testament is put on the manner of his death, as a criminal, on a cross; in short, it was a penal death. He was bearing penalty for sin—imposed by man unjustly, but imposed by God justly—for real sin, *ours*. It was therefore a "penal satisfaction" kind of atonement.

And in this the New Testament echoes the Old:

> But he was pierced for our transgressions,
>   he was crushed for our iniquities;
> the punishment that brought us peace
>   was upon him,
>   and by his wounds we are healed.
> We all, like sheep, have gone astray,
>   each of us has turned to his own way;
> and the LORD has laid on him
>   the iniquity of us all.
> …he poured out his life unto death,
>   and was numbered with the
>   transgressors.
> For he bore the sin of many,
>   and made intercession for the
>   transgressors
>   (Isa. 53:5-6, 12b).

The staggering truth is that Jesus in some very real sense experienced the pangs of the damned. As evidence we may mention again his cry of dereliction, his sense of being abandoned. It is shown in his agony in the Garden, when he pled for a way to escape, not physical death, but that awful deeper death, in which he would feel the guilt of a lost world.[7] Though not guilty, Jesus felt guilt. To bear our sin could mean nothing less. As Richard Howard says: "When Christ died on the Cross it was more than a physical death. It was a death *in relationship to sin*, a spiritual separation from his Father (cf. Rom. 6:10)."[8] It would be hard to escape the conclusion that on that middle cross occurred an experiencing of the pangs of the damned. Christ suffered a wrenching between his soul and the Father, and felt the horrible lostness of abandonment.

The importance of this for a doctrine of atonement is far-reaching. If the penalty for sin were solely physical death, then Jesus' mere experience of dying physically would have been sufficient. But if the penalty for sin is the wrath of God

---

[7]Speaking of Hebrews 5:7, Charles W. Carter reminds us that the phrase "save him from death" is "better understood as save Him 'out of death.'" He comments further: "This can hardly be correctly understood as a prayer for deliverance from death in Gethsemane, as if He were afraid of dying before He reached the cross" (*The Wesleyan Bible Commentary,* vol. VI, p. 73). And as already stated: Neither can his prayer be construed as a cry for avoidance of physical death on the cross. As horrible as such suffering was, it was no greater for him than for the thieves crucified on either side.

[8]*Newness of Life: A Study in the Thought of Paul* (Kansas City, MO: Beacon Hill Press, 1975), p. 101.

and the peril of the "second death" (eternal separation from God), an adequate atonement would require that Jesus represent us in that also. To "taste death for everyone" (Heb. 2:9) must mean far more than tasting the death of the body; it must mean entering into the very torments of hell and feeling the horror of spiritual condemnation and eternal lostness. The assurance voiced by the Psalmist and applied by Peter to Jesus, "you will not abandon me to the grave, nor will you let your Holy One see decay" (Acts 2:27; cf. 13:35), did not seem to be a conscious consolation during Jesus' agonizing struggle. His bearing of sin and its terrible increment was no charade; it was absolutely real.

Summary

When Adam and Eve disobeyed, they experienced death in its dual sense. Spiritual death occurred immediately, in its essential elements: alienation from God, and personal depravity. Physical death at once set in, though its fulfillment was mercifully extended hundreds of years. Physical death was both the natural consequence of their sin and the penal sanction on their sin.

The import of all this is that salvation is primarily from sin and its pollution, not from physical death. The Atonement does not save us *from* physical death. It makes possible our ultimate salvation *out* of death in the Resurrection. But the central stress in the New Testament is on the kind of death which separates us from God.

The penalty of sin therefore is twofold: physical and spiritual death. Just as the first result of sin in the Garden was spiritual death, with physical death following, so the primary benefit of the Atonement is salvation from sin, with resurrection following. In this life physical death is inescapable (Heb. 9:27). Only spiritual death can at this stage be remedied by regeneration and sanctification.

The peril to which the human race is still exposed, in spite of the Atonement, is the peril of allowing spiritual death to become eternal (the "second death"—Rev. 20:6, 14). Only personal appropriation of the merit of Christ's substitute death can save us from such a horrible fate.

6

Is Penalty a
Divine Necessity?

Many theologians have serious difficulty with the "penalty" question. Typical of the thinking of these persons is the bold announcement of an evangelist: "Christ did not die to appease an angry God, but to demonstrate the love of God." In the first part of the statement we have caricature, in the second part a half-truth. The caricature is the inaccurate twist given to the penal satisfaction theory of the Atonement; the second half is true but inadequate. By itself it proclaims the Moral Influence Theory.

Demolishing Straw Men

Very few have seriously interpreted the Atonement as a prying of mercy from a reluctant God. This is rather the straw man the Socinians and fellow travelers have delighted to erect, and equally delighted in demolishing. Appeasement smacks of buying a tyrant off. But satisfying a moral demand inherent in the nature of God is not appeasement. God's anger is his displeasure with sin, but a displeasure which acts.

The action is the gift of his Son as a means of satisfying the moral demands of holy wrath. But the gift was not only made necessary by the wrath, but an expression of love—the love of the Being who was wrathful. So both divine love and divine wrath are the source of the cross. As Elwood Sanner says: "In his identification with sinful man, Jesus became the object of God's wrath against sin."[1]

If love alone were at work here, unconditional forgiveness could have been extended to the whole world without such a horrible price as the suffering of God's only Son. But God is holy as well as loving, and holiness governs the way love functions. It is never a love ungoverned by holiness. Holiness requires that sin be costly; love bore the cost. But the cost was not borne by the Son alone, in order to persuade God the Father to be merciful. It was borne mutually by Father and Son—the Father as the initiating Giver, and the Son as the satisfying Sacrifice.

Again we hear: "God deals with sinners not according to justice but according to mercy." But it is heresy to proclaim that without adding, "Because justice was satisfied at Calvary." If the cross was not related to my sin at the point of justice, then why did God allow Jesus to die on it? If God spares us from justice just because he is merciful, then why would he not be equally merciful to his sinless Son?

It should become axiomatic in our thinking that the necessity of penalty is not incompatible with love. It was love that

---

[1]"Mark," *Beacon Hill Commentary*, vol. 6 (Kansas City, MO: Beacon Hill Press, 1964) p. 394. Sanner refers this statement to 2 Cor. 5:21; Mark 15:34.

gave God's only Son for our redemption; but it was the necessity of penalty that made the gift of his Son, not only necessary, but necessary as a blood sacrifice.

Necessity in God?

A more impressive (though not more profound) problem which some raise is the propriety of describing any particular form of atonement as a divine necessity. One writer comments: "We cannot even say that God could not have provided for atonement by a method other than death." He fears that to try to pin God down to one way of redeeming man is a form of "evangelical rationalism," which implies that God is not sovereign but is "subject to certain laws of necessity, as the ancient Stoics taught, about God."

This, of course, is the old debate between voluntarists and intellectualists, or the question of will vs. mind. Is what God does *right* simply because he wills it, or does God will it because it is *right*? H. Ray Dunning points out that John Wesley refused to get painted into such a corner, insisting that it was an artificial disjunction. "It seems, then, that the whole difficulty arises from considering God's will as distinct from God; Consequently, to say that the will of God, or that God himself, is the cause of the law, is one and the same thing."[2]

What this means for the question at issue is that in God, necessity and freedom are one. He always acts in harmony with his own perfections and always acts in total freedom. The mode of redemption by means of the death of his Son on a

---

[2]*Grace, Faith, and Holiness*, p. 196, quoting Wesley, "The Origin, Nature, Property, and Use of the Law," *Standard Sermons*, vol. 2, p. 50.

cross proceeded willingly yet necessarily from the depths of his holy and loving nature. This premise argues that God's love and nature acted in the only way possible. It was not only the best way, but a divine necessity. The historical fact that Christ was "handed over" to the Jews "by God's set purpose and foreknowledge" (Acts 2:23) is eloquent evidence that this exact event, and not some other, flowed necessarily from the composite of God's Being and Attributes. No other mode of redemption could have precisely expressed the loving and just holiness of God.

P.T. Forsyth is abundantly justified in declaring: "The more ethically we construe the Gospel the more we are driven upon the holiness of God. And the deeper we enter that sacred ground the more we are seized by the necessity (for the very maintenance of our spiritual life) of a real and objective atonement offered to a holy God by the equal and satisfying holiness of Christ under the conditions of sin and judgment."[3]

The sentence in the opening paragraph of chapter three will bear repeating: "The cruel death of God's Son on a cross, if some other way to save the human race would have worked equally well, is not only inconceivable, but would be indefensible."

Are God's Judgments Retributive?

To justify dispensing with punishment in explaining the Atonement made by Christ, some reject completely the con-

---

[3]*Positive Preaching and Modern Mind* (New York: George H. Doran Company, 1907), p. 373.

cept of retributive justice as an action of God in dealing with men and women. By retributive is meant action which is strictly penal in nature and purpose. These thinkers would opt for non-retributive action on God's part, by which is meant a kind of punishment or suffering which has as its goal not justice but correction. It is therefore utilitarian.

One of America's popular preachers, heard by millions, said: "God does not punish people. He never has and never will." Then he added: "We punish ourselves." This is to use the term punishment in a very loose sense, for punishment, strictly speaking, is the imposition of penalties for wrongdoing by a properly constituted governmental power.

The radio preacher's bald statement is similar to that of the young pastor who declared: "God is never angry with sinners." Neither preacher was very well acquainted with the Bible. "Therefore the LORD's anger burns against his people," declares Isaiah, "his hand is raised and he strikes them down" (Isa. 5:25). And Jesus "looked around at them in anger deeply distressed at their stubborn hearts" (Mark 3:5). A God, either as Father or Son, who did not get angry with evil would not be a good God. Such moral indifference would not make God superior but inferior—even to decent human beings.[4]

---

[4]Charles Colson says, "People have a greater fear of disease than of God's judgment." He blames this on a "low view of God." Schuller and others think that to preach a God of judgment is to present a low view of God. But as Harry Blamire says (quoted by Colson): "The real Christian Message must disturb.... There must be Heaven in the Christian Message, and there must be Hell." *The God of Stones and Spiders* (Wheaton, IL: Crossway Books, 1990), p. 99.

As far as punishing is concerned: that God does punish wrongdoers is taught so pervasively in the Bible that only rosetinted glasses could so egregiously miss the obvious.

Of course it could be said that even the "goats" who "will go away to eternal punishment" (Matt. 25:46), are sending themselves there, and therefore it is a kind of self-punishment. This is true, for we are the architects of our destiny. Even though God has declared his desire to save all of us, and has a benevolent design for each one, we can reject his plan and bring about our own destruction. For this we are solely to blame. Our eternal loss is a moral consequence of our rebellion. But Jesus calls the destiny of the "goats" a punishment, pronounced upon them by a Judge, "the Son of Man...[who] will sit on his throne in heavenly glory" (v. 31).

In the Old Testament, God warned the children of Israel that if they did not keep his covenant, "I myself will punish you for your sins seven times over" (Lev. 26:28). Through Isaiah the LORD says: "I will punish the world for its evil, the wicked for their sins" (13:11). That this is retributive is made clear in Isaiah 3:11: "Woe to the wicked! Disaster is upon them! They will be paid back for what their hands have done." What else but retributive could the following warning be also: "See, the LORD is coming out of his dwelling to punish the people of the earth for their sins" (Isa. 26:21). At least fifteen promises of punishment by God himself are found in Jeremiah.

So much for the claim that "God does not punish persons. He never has and never will."

It is possible that the speaker meant that God does not punish directly, only indirectly, by creating a moral order in which wrong-doing brings its own pain and righteousness brings its own reward. That we are in such a moral order is without doubt. But to imply that this is the extent of any punishment which occurs is to imply a *deistic* world view—that God created the universe with its natural and moral laws and simply allows these laws to function unaided and without interference. This, of course, is not the God of the Bible. The Bible from cover to cover presents a God who is not only transcendent but immanent; a God not only of created law but of personal and immediate involvement; involvement not only as Father and Savior but as Moral Governor who judges his people. This is the theism of the Bible, and therefore of the Christian religion.

While Arminian theologians would repudiate any such form of deism, some of them also are stressing the disciplinary nature of punishment rather than its retributive nature. One writer says: "Punishment is corrective in purpose.... Those lost in hell are not being punished, for in that place there is no hope of correction."[5] This implies a quite arbitrary definition of punishment as primarily disciplinary which is unsupportable by either the dictionary or the Bible. That punishment, as e.g. parental, is often corrective and disciplinary in purpose is of course true. But that discipline is the primary meaning and purpose of punishment *per se* is not true.

---

[5]Charles Carter, *Life's Lordship Over Death* (Indianapolis: Wesley Press, 1988), stated in Introduction by Wayne E. Caldwell, p. viii.

Punishment is the imposition of a penalty for misconduct, without necessary regard to the punishment's beneficent or non-beneficent effects.

That this hard side of retribution cannot be ruled out of the divine economy is made clear from such passages as 2 Thessalonians 1:6-9: "God is just: He will pay back trouble to those who trouble you...He will punish those who do not know God and do not obey the gospel of our Lord Jesus. They will be punished with everlasting destruction." The word here is *diken tio,* "to pay justice." This is purely retributive, without any thought of redemption; in fact, redemption is explicitly ruled out.

Nor is there hope of redemption being held out in Hebrews 10:28-29: "Anyone who rejected the law of Moses died without mercy on the testimony of two or three witnesses. How much more severely do you think a man deserves to be punished who has trampled the Son of God under foot, who has treated as an unholy thing the blood of the covenant?..."

Retributive punishment, without ultimate redemption, is also declared by Paul in Romans 2:5-6: "But because of your stubbornness and your unrepentant heart, you are storing up wrath against yourself for the day of God's wrath, when his righteous judgment will be revealed. God will give to each person according to what he has done" (cf. Ps.62:12).

C. S. Lewis has some trenchant things to say about the anti-retributive theory of punishment: "The Humanitarian theory removes from Punishment the concept of Desert. But the concept of Desert is the only connecting link between punishment and justice. It is only as deserved or undeserved that a sentence can be just or unjust".[6] He goes on to point out that in the long run, to treat human beings in any other way than as they deserve is to dehumanize them and make them mere cogs or things. They cease to be responsible, morally accountable human beings. Mercy is not justified if it waives justice purely for mercy's sake. To apply this to the Atonement: God allowed Christ to be treated as a sinner deserves, in order that mercy towards us could be compatible with justice.

Forgiveness Without Atonement?

Some Scriptures seem to indicate that forgiveness flows out of God's nature, with or without an atonement. "You are forgiving and good, O Lord, abounding in love to all who call on you" (Ps. 86:5). Then the psalmist adds: "But you, O Lord, are a compassionate and gracious God, slow to anger, abounding in love and faithfulness" (v. 15). When God revealed himself to Moses, it was as "The LORD, the LORD, the compassionate and gracious God, slow to anger, abounding in love and faithfulness, maintaining love to thousands, and forgiving wickedness, rebellion and sin" (Exod. 34:6,7). At this Moses, "bowed to the ground at once and worshiped. 'O Lord, if I have found favor in your eyes,' he said, 'then let the Lord go with us. Although this is a stiff-necked people, forgive our wickedness and our sin, and take us as your inheritance'"(vv. 8,9).[7]

---

[6]*God in the Dock*, Walter Hooper, ed. (Grand Rapids: William B. Eerdmans Publishing Company, 1970), p. 287ff.

[7]Cf. Neh. 9:17; Ps. 103:8; 145:8; Joel 2:13; John 4:2.

Similar inferences can be found in the New Testament as, for instance, in the case of the Prodigal Son. The calf was slain for a feast, but no blood was shed for atonement as a basis on which the father would receive his son back.

But as proof that atoning blood is after all not absolutely essential, all these testimonies to God's loving heart collapse before the declaration of one verse: Jesus is "the Lamb that was slain from the creation of the world" (Rev. 13:8b). Supporting this is Peter's declaration that we are redeemed "with the precious blood of Christ," who "was chosen before the creation of the world, but was revealed in these last times" (1 Pet. 1:19-20; cf. Eph. 1:4). This silences forever the sanguine notion of easy forgiveness. For all the declarations of God's love and mercy are made against the backdrop of a stark cross, already in place in the mind and plan of God.

What is the real ground of faith in God? Is it not the evidence found in the Scripture and experienced in life that his love is holy? As holy, it is not only steadfast but righteous. There is integrity in God's love. God will keep his word. God will do what he says he will do. Unless we see this quality in a person, is trust possible? Emotional expressions of love are a poor foundation for trust. But when we learn that a person is reliable, that he keeps his word, then trust is solidly grounded. Faith is rooted in a consistent and invariable demonstration of word-keeping.

It is Calvary which makes trust in God possible, not because Calvary is a demonstration of God's love—though it is that—but because it is a proof of God's integrity. God said that sin would bring death. In Christ hanging on the cross, we see God keeping his word.

The implications of such a penal theory are that the sinner (1) be treated as he deserves, and (2) in harmony with God's own sanctions against sin. Death was declared in advance as the penalty for sin. Therefore any possible atonement must serve the purpose of penalty. In so doing, the Atonement would vindicate God's integrity. Thus, to reiterate, the deepest note respecting the sufferings of Christ is that they were penal in nature.

7

The Blood Imperative

It has often been observed that running through the Bible is a scarlet thread. It begins in the Garden, when skins were required to replace fig leaves. It is seen in the sacrifice of Abel. Some would deny that this bears on the question of blood atonement.[1] But the biblical evidence is hard to refute. According to Hebrews 11:4, Abel was assured of his justification before God, not because he was a better man, but because "he offered God a better sacrifice."[2] Cain's offering was reject-

---

[1] For a pro and con discussion by Herschel H. Hobbs and Joel D. Heck, see *The Genesis Debate*, Ronald Youngblood, ed. (New York: Thomas Nelson, Publisher, 1986), p. 130.

[2] The NIV is very unsatisfactory here. Abel was not "commended as a righteous man," as if he were being praised for what he already was by his own efforts, and therefore didn't really need a propitiatory sacrifice; rather "he obtained the testimony that he was righteous, God testifying about his gifts"(NASB): God was not testifying about his prior character but about the superiority of his offering, and on the basis of that declared Abel righteous. Furthermore, the NIV ascribes the witness to his righteousness directly to his faith, whereas it was by faith that he offered the better sacrifice through which he obtained the witness. See A.T. Robertson, *Word Pictures in the New Testament*, vol.1, p. 419.

ed, not because what he offered was shoddy or unacceptable in some circumstances, but because he was trifling with sin. "If you do what is right," God said, "will you not be accepted?" (Gen 4:7). Where there is no sin, the products of our own culture are appropriate offerings to God in worship. But sin radically alters the relationship of the worshiper to God. His sin blocks his acceptance (Isa. 59:1-2). If contact is going to be made with God, sin must be faced, acknowledged, and atoned for. From Genesis to Revelation, the Bible confirms the thesis that only blood can atone for sin.

Biblically Pervasive

Why blood shedding is so basic will become clearer to us as we pursue our survey. But first, the fact that blood is required must be established. Here in the first four chapters of Genesis are two examples. The evidence is cumulative. The presupposition of blood sacrifice as the proper approach to God on the part of sinners is seen in Noah's sacrifice following the flood (Gen. 8:20). There were also the numerous animal sacrifices of Abraham, Isaac, and Jacob. Isaac, even as a lad, understood the necessity of blood as he asked, "The fire and wood are here…where is the lamb?" (Gen. 22:7).

When we come to the Mosaic era, we have first the Passover event, with God's words: "When I see the blood, I will pass over you" (Exod. 12:13). As for the cultus established in the wilderness, it was organized around the shedding of blood. The Sinaitic covenant was ratified by blood. All types of offerings, including the burnt offering, required the killing of an animal. The only exception was in the case of extreme poverty, in which case the penitent was permitted to bring "a tenth of an ephah of fine flour" (Lev. 5:11-13). Normally the blood requirement was ubiquitous. The elaborate system of atonement, which controlled the religious life of the nation daily, weekly, on special feast occasions, and then annually on the Great Day of Atonement, caused virtually "rivers" of blood to flow, first in the wilderness camp and later in the temple. As onerous as the burden must have been both for worshipers and ministering Levites and priests, the blood nevertheless kept flowing.

Notwithstanding the burden, according to the biblical record the entire complex sacrificial system was imposed on the Israelites by God himself. Only the reading of the Old Testament with the extremely biased eye of liberalism could miss this note of divine authority. Gleason L. Archer declares: "Nothing could be clearer than that this entire sacrificial system was no invention of the Hebrew people (either in Moses' day or in the course of later centuries) but a direct revelation of God. Otherwise no affirmation of divine origin is to be trusted for any statement in the rest of Scripture."[3]

---

[3]*A Survey of Old Testament Introduction* (Chicago: Moody Press, 1964), p. 228.

While a few psalms and prophetic passages seem to deprecate blood sacrifices, a closer look will see clearly that their thrust is against the presumption of supposing that the system can be pleasing to God in detachment from the fidelity and obedience of the people. The rebukes of the prophets were frequently needed to call the nation back to the spiritual meaning and the moral obligation implicit in the blood. The multiplication of sacrifices was odious to God if it merely masqueraded their hypocrisy and disloyalty. God was angry when he

Equally In the New Testament

But the pervasiveness of the blood did not end with the Old Testament. It finds its full counterpart, indeed its *interface*, in the New. No matter how the New Testament writers refer to the death of Christ, "the background of thought," says Stott, "is still the Old Testament sacrificial system."[4] Not only does the typological significance of all the sacrifices, ceremonies, and special days converge on One Person, the Lord Jesus Christ, but the emphasis on the blood is not altered, shifted, or lessened. Indeed, Jesus went much farther than Moses. Moses had ingrained in the Israelites a horror of eating blood or anything with blood in it. Jesus faced these very Israelites and alienated them by the shocking ultimatum: "I

---

was compelled to exclaim: "These people come near to me with their mouth and honor me with their lips, but their hearts are far from me" (Isa. 29:13; cf. Hosea 8:12-13; Amos 5:21-23; Isa.1:12-16). As R. Larry Shelton observes, "Correct observance of the covenant ritual was important, but the covenant relationship was maintained by Israel's moral correspondence to the will of Yahweh as expressed in his word at Sinai." "Initial Salvation," *A Contemporary Wesleyan Theology*, vol. 1 (Grand Rapids: Francis Asbury Press, 1983), p. 481.

This means that without humility, repentance, and fidelity in their worship, the entire system degenerated into superstition; the same kind that has often gathered around the sacraments. The problem of routine without worship, form without heart, and rites which do not result in righteousness, seems to be a perennial one. It is the illusion of benefit which depends solely on the technical niceties of correct performance. It is the false security of a mechanical routine, like the turning of a prayer wheel—remarkably like the supposition of some Christians that Christ's blood always covers, whether or not those who "trust" in it are being faithful to it.

[4]John R.W. Stott, *The Cross of Christ*, p. 134.

tell you the truth, unless you eat the flesh of the Son of Man and drink his blood, you have no life in you" (John 6:53). Later, in the Upper Room, when inaugurating the Lord's Supper, Jesus said as he passed the cup, "Drink from it, all of you." Then he adds: "This is my blood of the covenant" (Matt. 26:28).

In view of the very natural human repugnance toward a blood-centered religion—the kind of repugnance which has prompted many moderns to delete the blood from their hymnals—one would suppose that the Early Church would have modified this sharp focus.[5] It would have been easy for them to tone down this strange concentration. But the New Testament does not bear out such an expectation. It is through "faith in his blood" that we are to be saved (Rom. 3:25). We are "now justified by his blood" (Rom. 5:9). According to Paul's letter to the Ephesians, "we have redemption through his blood" (1:7) and we are "made nigh by the blood of Christ" (2:13). The same affirmations are made in almost identical terms in Colossians (1:14, 20). The blood theme is introduced by Peter in his First Epistle in his first sentence; and in 1:18-19 he says: "For you know that it was not with perishable things such as silver or gold that you were redeemed...but with the precious blood of Christ, a lamb without blemish or defect." According to John, if we walk in

---

[5]Typical of profound antipathy toward the idea of blood is the statement of J.D.G. Dunn: "Many of the NT metaphors and analogies are archaic and distasteful to modern sensibilities (e.g., blood sacrifice)." "Demythologizing—The Problem of Myth in the New Testament," in *New Testament Interpretation*, p. 345.

the light, "the blood of Jesus, his [God's] Son, purifies us from all sin" (1 John 1:7). In Revelation we read that Christ has "freed us from our sins by his blood" (1:5) and that the worshipers around the throne "sang a new song":

> 'You are worthy to take the scroll and to open
> its seals, because you were slain, and with your
> blood you purchased men for God' (5:9).

As for the epistle to the Hebrews, it is the classic exposition of the blood of Christ as being the great antitype toward which every drop of blood shed under Moses pointed. When Jesus fulfilled his office as High Priest, it was in the heavenly tabernacle, and "He did not enter by means of the blood of goats and calves, but he entered the Most Holy Place once for all by his own blood" (9:12).

Earlier it was said that the Bible teaching from Genesis to Revelation is that only blood atones for sin. The declaration of Hebrews 9:22 is unambiguous: "In fact, the law requires that nearly everything be cleansed with blood, and without the shedding of blood there is no forgiveness." We are compelled to admit that the shedding of blood is as central in the New Testament scheme of things as it most certainly was in the Old Testament; but now it is Christ's blood which is the focus, and in which is the culmination and fulfillment of everything practiced under the Law.

Why Blood?

It will be helpful to examine again the case of Cain and Abel in order to delve more deeply into the question, "Why blood?" We need to establish that Abel as well as Cain was a sinner and needed to be justified. This fact can best be confirmed by bringing the teachings of the New Testament to bear on these brothers, just as Jesus interpreted to the two on the road to Emmaus the Old Testament in terms of himself. If, as Augustine said, "the New Testament is in the Old concealed and the Old Testament is in the New revealed," we will find that principle here, if anywhere.[6] The New Testament position unequivocally is that all are sinners and all need atonement for their sins. It cannot be that we are to take the New Testament seriously in its diagnosis of the human situation for the first century, and not see it as a timeless assertion about fallen humanity from Adam forward. Therefore Abel and Cain as well as all others in their day and all others since have needed atonement for sin.

It is true that 1 John 3:12 states that Cain's actions were evil and Abel's "were righteous." This may imply a difference in character between the two brothers, based on personal decision and adopted principles. While all are sinners needing atonement, some are relatively righteous just as others are especially wicked. However, the writer to the Hebrews makes it clear that it was the superiority of his sacrifice that secured

---

[6]Gerhard von Rad reminds us: "We have the undeniable fact that so very often even the best 'historical' exegesis is achieved from a theological point of view—that is to say, in the final analysis, from the side of the Christian faith." "Typological Interpretation of the Old Testament," *A Guide to Contemporary Hermeneutics: Major Trends in Biblical Interpretation*, Donald K. McKim, ed. (Grand Rapids: William B. Eerdmans Publishing Company, 1986), p. 44.

for Abel God's approval of his offering and the witness to his righteousness. We are not permitted to conclude that Abel's own prior righteousness was the reason for God accepting his offering, and that the offering itself had nothing to do with the divine declaration of his righteousness. For the assumption of the biblical sacrificial system was that blood sacrifices served to provide a basis for acceptability with God. If Abel had been a perfect paragon of virtue, having no sin needing atonement, then there is no reason he could not have approached God without any offering at all. We cannot escape the plain inference in Hebrews, which states that it was "through" the "better sacrifice" that Abel "obtained the testimony that he was righteous, God testifying about his gifts"; that is, God endorsed the gifts as being adequate to provide a basis for Abel's justification.

Now Cain's offering would have been acceptable in some circumstances. Under the Mosaic system there was a grain offering. It was called the peace offering; sometimes the fellowship offering. But it didn't come first; it came after the blood sacrifices. Sin had to be expiated first; then grain offerings were in order. This was exactly what God said to Cain: "If you do what is right, will you not be accepted? But if you do not do what is right, sin is crouching at your door; it desires to have you, but you must master it" (Gen. 4:7). Here was not only guilt for wrongdoing, but a sinful, jealous nature, which had to be restrained or would lead to murder—which it did.

The problem then with Cain was that he either failed to see the hideous malady of sin, either in act or spirit; or, seeing it, presumed on the mercy of God. But we cannot presume on

God's mercy in the presence of the sin for which no atonement is made.[7]

Now we reach the bedrock principle. Abel was not justified simply by exercising faith in a good and merciful God. Abel was justified by offering by faith a kind of sacrifice, in distinction from Cain's, that made it morally justifiable for a holy God to forgive sin.

God cannot justly forgive sin simply because he is a good-natured and amiable God. God yearns to be merciful, but he is not good-natured and amiable—not in the presence of sin. God is holy, and holiness will not allow good-natured amiability where sin is. Sin is an affront to God. Sin is too serious for a holy God to be good-natured about it. God must deal with sin, and his dealing with sin must match its seriousness. He declared at the beginning that sin would bring death—spiritual and physical. And just as physical death means separation from a temporal environment, so spiritual death means separation, even alienation, from man's true home, his spiritual environment.

God cannot simply excuse the sinner from the consequences of his sin. As Stott puts it, "God must not only respect us for the responsible beings we are, but he must also respect himself for the holy God he is."[8] There must be a suffering of

---

[7]Commenting on Jude 11, "They have taken the way of Cain," E. M. Blaiklock says: "Cain was the symbol of carnality in worship. His graceful altar, flower-decked, was the emblem of the easy path, of religion stripped of sternness and austerity." *The Compact Handbook of New Testament Life* (Minneapolis: Bethany House Publishers, 1979), p. 124.

[8]*The Cross of Christ*, p. 116.

sin's ill-deserts, either by the sinner, which would mean eternal hopelessness, or by a representative in his behalf. When the full gravity of sin is demonstrated by a death which is penal in nature, and if that death is willingly and worthily experienced in behalf of, and in the place of, the sinner himself, God can justly free the sinner from the proper consequences of his sin on the basis of this satisfaction.

Abel was too close to the original Garden tragedy not to understand this. Therefore, if we ask what there was about Abel's sacrifice which made it more acceptable than Cain's, we answer: Blood. Blood speaks of the penal desert of sin, and blood represents a penal satisfaction; a satisfaction by way of substitution—the innocent lamb for guilty Abel.

Of course it is understood that all the animal blood which flowed from Adam to the temple sacrifices in Christ's day could not in and of itself wipe out a single sin. Its acceptability lay solely in its function as symbolic (in the mind of God) of that holy blood which was to flow at Calvary. The writer to the Hebrews makes it clear that in the ultimate sense, "it is impossible for the blood of bulls and goats to take away sins" (Heb. 10:4). It could only serve the duty of type, temporarily acceptable to God as a token cleansing, thus avoiding immediate judgment, until the antitype appeared with blood sufficient to counterbalance all sin. And the animal blood was efficacious only by pointing to One whose blood, while like animal blood in a crass physiological way, was also the blood of infinite deity incarnated. It was therefore a once-for-all substitute for the sinner's blood—the blood representing the death which the sinner deserved.

The Word explains:

> Not through the blood of goats and calves, but through his [Jesus'] own blood, he entered the holy place once for all, having obtained eternal redemption. For if the blood of goats and bulls and the ashes of a heifer sprinkling those who have been defiled, sanctify for the cleansing of the flesh, how much more will the blood of Christ, who through the eternal Spirit offered himself without blemish to God, cleanse your conscience from dead works to serve the living God? (Heb. 9:12-14, NASB).

How inescapably clear it is therefore that Christ's blood served the same function, but in absolute, final, and perfect measure, which animal blood served in the Old Testament order. This means that the blood of Christ was propitiatory in nature, satisfying that in the divine nature which required retribution; which is to say that it was penal in nature. The shed blood of Christ answered to the demand for justice; and in so doing became the means of mercy.

What the blood meant in the Old Testament therefore is what it means in the New, but to a perfect and consummating degree. Blood for Old Testament worshipers was the prescribed means of approaching a holy God. The blood was for atonement—i.e., a means of obtaining God's mercy, of re-affirming the covenant, of escaping divine wrath, and experiencing both ceremonial holiness and a measure of spiritual peace. But what the blood of animals achieved in shadow, Jesus' blood achieved in substance. "How much more, then, will the blood of Christ,…cleanse our consciences from acts that lead to death, so that we may serve the living God!" (Heb. 9:14). Jesus "suffered outside the city gate to make the people holy through his own blood" (Heb. 13:12).

Blood—Death or Life?

The taboo against eating blood was explained by God as having a twofold significance: First, "the life of a creature is in the blood" (Lev. 17:11, 14; cf. Deut. 12:3). By analogy, God thus taught the Israelites the sanctity of human life. But more important was the second reason: "I have given it to you to make atonement for yourselves on the altar; it is the blood that makes atonement for one's life" (Lev. 17:11b). Elsewhere the universal note is that the blood makes atonement for one's sin. Here the word is "life." The connection cannot be missed. One's sin takes one's life as hostage. The sentence of death is attached to one's life, unless it can be lifted by a blood atonement. Here is strong intimation that the blood shedding is penal in nature. It is a means of propitiating a holy God and providing for the expiation of sin. This passage, says Stott, is the "clearest statement that the blood sacrifices of the Old Testament ritual had a substitutionary significance."[9]

The life which is jeopardized is first of all physical life, for Israelites who disregarded their sins and failed or refused to participate in blood sacrifices were to be "cut off"—put to death. But in the deeper sense, the life identified in Leviticus was spiritual and eternal; for the separating power of sin is far more than simply the jeopardy to physical life; it has no other

---

[9]Ibid., p. 137.

means of being cancelled or its eternal consequences annulled than blood sacrifices.

Following the lead of B.F. Westcott, some scholars have seized upon these passages to develop the peculiar thesis that the meaningful note in the sacrificial shedding of blood was not death, but the releasing of life. Symbolically it signified making the life of the animal, and then the life of Christ, available to the believer. It was Christ's means of transmitting his life to humans. But James Denney has no patience with this. He says, "I venture to say that a more groundless fancy never haunted and troubled the interpretation of any part of Scripture."[10] John R.W. Stott believes that Alan Stibbs put this fancy to rest in his monograph, *The Meaning of the Word 'Blood' in Scripture*, by establishing the thesis that "blood" in the Scriptures is a word-symbol for death.[11] Of Westcott's theory, Leon Morris says: "This view is not adequate...It does

---

[10]*The Death of Christ*, p. 274. On p. 284 Denney declares: "To preach the love of God out of relation to the death of Christ—or to preach the love of God in the death of Christ, but without being able to relate it to sin—or to preach the forgiveness of sins as the free gift of God's love, while the death of Christ has no special significance assigned to it— is not, if the New Testament is the rule and standard of Christianity, to preach the gospel at all."

[11]*The Cross of Christ*, p. 180. Stibbs concludes his monograph by stating: "To drink his blood' means not to appropriate His life, nor to feed upon His glorified humanity, nor to draw upon the power of His resurrection—with the Cross put into the background as but a necessary preliminary to release the life. Rather does it mean consciously, and by faith alone, humbly to appropriate all our blessings, and not least redemption and cleansing from sin, as wholly and solely the benefits of His death." *The Meaning of the Word 'Blood' in Scripture* (London: The Tyndale Press, 1948), p. 31.

not square with the repeated affirmation that sacrifice is 'to make atonement.'"[12]

The Rock On Which Governmentalism Breaks

This consistent emphasis on blood in the Bible in both Testaments poses real problems for the advocates of a solely governmental theory of the Atonement. For the emphasis affirms a continuity between Christ's death and the Mosaic sacrificial system, which is declared consistently to provide an atonement for sin. The blood was not simply a means of worship, or a means of proclaiming the justice of God governmentally (or even, primarily, the means of ratifying a covenant), but a means first, *of getting right with God*, and second, of maintaining an acceptable relationship with God.

The point which now needs to be made is this: If Christ's blood was not primarily penal in nature and directly a means of satisfying the moral and legal claims against the sinner, but rather merely a means of proclaiming God's wrath against sin for the sake of upholding moral government, then the connection between Christ's death and the Old Testament breaks down. The continuity between his blood and the shedding of blood in the Old Testament disappears. The New Testament,

---

[12]*Baker's Dictionary of Theology* (1960), p. 467. He says: "In modern times an idea has sprung up that the essential thing in sacrifice is not the infliction of death as sin's penalty, but the presentation of life before God. The worshiper's life may not be thus presented because it is stained with sin, but God graciously permits him to substitute the life of the animal" (and by implication, the life of Christ). Morris takes the same position in his *Cross in the New Testament.*

in this case, would be in the anomalous position of adopting the same focus on the blood, and the same terminology, but with radically different meaning.

The epistle to the Hebrews also provides the final answer to the notion that the Mosaic sacrifices were really not ordained of God; and at any rate did not carry the meaning of penal satisfaction. The writer identifies the Septuagint version of Psalm 40:6-8 as the assignment with which Christ identified when he came into this world:

> Sacrifice and offering you did not desire,
>   but a body you prepared for me;
> with burnt offerings and sin offerings
>   you were not pleased.
> Then I said, 'Here I am—it is written
>   about me in the scroll—
> I have come to do your will, O God.'
>   (Heb. 10:5-7)

The writer immediately makes clear that this "body" was not merely the form which the Incarnation took as a means of revealing the Father, but was a body which could be offered in blood sacrifice. Because they were inadequate, all other "bodies"—those of animals—were in themselves distasteful to God ("although the law required them to be made," v. 8), and could only serve to provide a temporary patchwork covering until the Great Sacrifice to which they pointed came; then were to be done away with totally. "He sets aside the first to establish the second" (v. 9). By "that will we have been made holy through the sacrifice of the body of Jesus Christ once for all" (v. 10).

It was the physical body of Jesus which took the place of animals, because it had blood in it to shed. It was the taking of this body for the purpose of shedding this blood that Christ came into the world. And the Word expressly declares that this action was the "will" of God. It was not a fluke. God ordained the Mosaic system, but only as a stopgap arrangement until the body of Christ could be offered as the final and eternal sacrifice, displacing and terminating all other sacrifices forever. But the fundamental point must not be missed: What the blood of animals provided—atonement for sin—was precisely what Christ's blood was shed to provide, but in perfect and final reality rather than in shadow. What the ancient high priests did once a year in entering the Most Holy Place to make atonement, Christ did once for all and finally, not "by means of the blood of goats and calves; but…by his own blood"(Heb. 9:12).

The orthodox dogma is: *The wages of sin is death; either the sinner must die or a substitute must die.* The "scarlet thread" which is indeed woven throughout the Scriptures would seem to confirm this dogma. Constantly the Old Testament speaks of blood sacrifice as a means of atonement. How could blood effect atonement if the blood did not represent a substitutionary death? But if substitutionary, could it be other than penal? It was needed because of sin and sins. Sin brought the offender under the death sentence. The sinner's hope was in allowing the animal to bear the death sentence in his or her place. That is *penal satisfaction.* Surely the death of Christ could have meant no less.

We cannot concede to those who would direct us down a side-path here, by claiming that the fundamental purpose of blood in the Old Testament was simply as an initial and then repeated ratification of God's covenant with his people. That the Sinaitic covenant was ratified with blood is of course recorded in the Scripture (Exod. 20-24). But that this provides the full meaning of blood in the Old Testament is contradicted by much more pervasive identification, in dozens of ways, of the blood as a necessary means of atoning for sin and setting the worshiper right with God. The covenant emphasis has been seized upon by some as an escape from the penal nature of the system. But it will not do.

While Jesus, in instituting the Lord's Supper, said, "This is my blood of the covenant," he immediately added, "which is poured out for many for the forgiveness of sins" (Matt. 26:28). The epistle to the Hebrews expounds thoroughly the nature of this covenant, as a provision for not only a new kind of acquaintance with God and total forgiveness of sins, but the writing of God's law on the hearts of those within the covenant—a covenant only made possible by the shedding of atoning blood. And so Jesus puts the emphasis right there: His outpoured blood was necessary for the forgiveness of sins. No stronger statement of substitutionary blood, as a necessary means of making forgiveness possible, could be made.[13]

---

[13]Archer puts it clearly: "The basic principle underlying all the blood sacrifices…was atonement (*kippur*) by the substitution of an innocent life for the guilty. In token of this substitution the offerer laid his hand upon the victim's head, thus identifying himself with it as his representative. To signify his acceptance of the just penalty of death, he himself slew his victim, and then turned it over to the priest for the completion of the ceremony" (*Survey*, p. 231).

8

Toward a Resolution

It is the conviction of this writer that Wesleyan/Arminians can come to terms with the penal satisfaction nature of the Atonement without accepting the objectionable baggage which has often accompanied it. We will first take time for a review of perspectives.

Review of Perspectives

Those who espouse the Governmental Theory grant the necessity of penalty. But their theory holds that Christ's death served the purpose of penalty by a public display of God's wrath against sin, for the upholding of universal law. It was therefore penal in a symbolic or token sense. Thus the sufferings of Christ, while fulfilling the purpose of penalty, were in their nature a substitute for penalty.

This special view of the penal nature of Christ's death differs from the usual Calvinistic view, which maintains that Christ fully in his own person bore our personal guilt, with its liability to punishment under divine wrath. They understand this vicarious bearing of guilt to be so absolute that no further bearing of guilt by the elect is possible. Lurking always in the background of the absolutistic position are the divine decrees, which of necessity invest the Atonement in respect to the elect with infallible effectiveness.[1] In such a system there is no room for any degree of true contingency or conditionality. On this basis it is quite logical to say that no further bearing of guilt—under wrath—is possible. Every sin, past, present, and future is already expiated.[2]

The difference between this position and the viewpoint argued in this book may seem like a fine line—but it is a "continental divide" kind of fine line. Whereas Calvinists see this vicarious bearing of our guilt as absolute, we see it as a satisfaction only for those who accept it in freedom.

Some of us as Wesleyans insist that Christ *did* bear the penalty, but believe that the principle of "double jeopardy" does not apply in a rigid, legalistic manner. The bearing of penalty on our behalf is annulled by unbelief, rejection, and persistent impenitence; and *equally* by a reversion to unbelief and impenitence.

The principle of "double jeopardy" is indeed a valid comfort for those who are *in* Christ, *now*, not simply at some

---

[1]Consistent Calvinists of the Synod of Dort type would say that the bond which imposed responsibility on Christ was the Covenant made unilaterally with his people by God, as the structure of his eternal decrees. All of the unabridged doctrines of hyper-Calvinism are herewith implied, including limited atonement. But the Bible says Christ died for the world, not for a pre-determined group within a covenant.

[2]A belief dear to the heart of contemporary Calvinists. For its more complete refutation see my *The Scandal of Pre-Forgiveness* (Salem, OH: Schmul Publishing Company, Inc., 1993).

point in the past. They too, with Paul, are "convinced that neither death nor life, neither angels nor demons, neither the present nor the future, nor any powers, neither height nor depth, nor anything else in all creation, will be able to separate us from the love of God that is in Christ Jesus our Lord" (Rom. 8:37-39). But continued willful sinning turns Christ's blood into compounded condemnation. Vicarious satisfaction must be accepted by the sinner not only by faith, but by the kind of faith that is honorable. To presume on the blood is to desecrate it.

There are still other objections in the minds of Wesleyan/Arminians to the penal satisfaction understanding. One, they object to the idea of Christ being "punished" since he was not personally guilty. Two, the problem of forgiveness still sticks in the craw of many. If Christ's death is a penal satisfaction—i.e., if Jesus really "paid it all"—wherein is there need for forgiveness?

How do Arminians handle these issues? One way, as we have seen, is by denying the absolute necessity of imposing punishment on the sinner. John Miley says: The infliction of penalty "in punishment is not an absolute necessity to the ends of its office."[3] God in his sovereignty can substitute a kind of atonement which does not involve a literal bearing of punishment.

Yet all the evidence so far, and certainly the position which seems to reach the deepest depths of both sin and holiness,

---

[3]*Systematic Theology*, vol. II (New York: Methodist Book Concern, 1894), p. 69.

points to the bedrock foundation premise that Christ's death was profoundly penal in nature, related directly to the demerit of our sin. How is this impasse to be resolved?

Making matters still more interesting is the fact that Miley and other governmentalists have departed from their denominational father, John Wesley. H. Ray Dunning concedes that Wesley adopted or at least used "the formulations of some form of the satisfaction theory."[4] This is somewhat of an embarrassment to contemporary Wesleyans, for to them he was seeming to endorse a theory of the Atonement which was at odds with his soteriology, including the universality and at the same time the conditionality of the Atonement's provisions.

Wesley's writings are sprinkled with such declarations as: "Art thou unable to atone for the least of thy sins? 'He is the propitiation for' all thy sins";[5] "*So loved us*, as to deliver up his only Son to die a cursed death for our salvation";[6] "How wonderfully was he manifested to angels and men, when he 'was wounded for our transgressions'; when he 'bore all our sins in his own body on the tree'; when, having 'by that one oblation of himself once offered, made a full, perfect, and sufficient sacrifice, oblation, and satisfaction for the sins of the whole world,' he cried out, 'It is finished; and bowed his head, and gave up the ghost!'"[7] The reference to "that one oblation" is substantially taken from the Articles of the Church of

---

[4]*Grace, Faith, and Holiness*, p. 334.
[5]*Works*, 5:257.
[6]*Works*, 6:235.
[7]*Works*, 6:274.

England, obviously being quoted with endorsement. The Methodist Articles of Religion, drawn up in 1784 by Wesley himself, contains the following: Christ was "crucified, dead and buried, to reconcile the Father to us, and to be a sacrifice, not only for original guilt, but also for the actual sins of men"; and "The offering of Christ, once made, is that perfect redemption, propitiation, and satisfaction for all the sins of the whole world, both original and actual; and there is none other satisfaction for sin but that alone."[8] Obviously Wesley had no qualms about either the word "propitiation" or the word "satisfaction."

Could it be that Wesley's theological instincts were sounder than those of his theological progeny?

Penalty or Punishment?

Perhaps the stumbling block is in failing to distinguish between punishment and penalty. Some things are absolutely non-transferable, such as virtue, holiness, guilt, demerit, and punishment. But penalty, as well as liability to suffering, is transferable. While Christ's sufferings in our behalf could not accurately be called punishments—for undeserved punishment is injustice—they may truly constitute the suffering of the penalty for sin which we deserved to bear.

This assumes that penalty may be defined as a legally established specific retribution for specific misdeeds. The bearing of such penalties by substitutes, who are not themselves guilty or properly punishable, is not unknown in the annals of law.

---

[8]Philip Schaff, *The Creeds of Christendom*, vol. III (Grand Rapids: Baker Book House, 1969), pp. 807, 811.

God pronounced the penalty of death upon sin. The sinless Son went to the Cross to take upon himself this penalty in real and sufficient measure, certainly in its physical dimension, and in some adequate sense in its spiritual dimension, in behalf of Adam and every sinner since.

That which differentiates this from the governmental understanding is the distinction between suffering a representative death to satisfy public justice, upholding "law and order," and satisfying the penal obligation of the individual sinner. The death of Christ was primarily related to my sin, personally, as a satisfaction of the law's claims against *me*, only secondarily as a public vindication of God's law. It is this which makes it at root a "penal satisfaction."

But, as has already been pointed out, this kind of substitution does not carry with it the kind of "double jeopardy" security which many have attached to it. We must continue to strike home the fact that it is a substitution which is relative, not absolute, because it is conditional. The Plan all along had within it, declared in one way or another consistently from the beginning, the element of conditionality. Christ's death was sufficient to cover in full the penalty for all who meet the moral conditions universally declared. The condition primarily is faith, but a kind of faith which is born of repentance and proceeds with obedience.

Penalty and Forgiveness

Then there is the second problem, that of forgiveness. How can there be the bearing of penalty at the cross and personal forgiveness both? How can I claim to be personally "forgiven" if there is nothing to forgive because the penalty is paid? This is a commercial/judicial notion which misses completely the moral dynamics of our relationship to God. There is only a fanciful conflict between singing "Jesus paid it all," then asking God for forgiveness and believing that he does forgive. Christ's death is penal in nature, and as such is potentially sufficient for the entire world. But it constitutes an umbrella under which I must choose to seek shelter. His death becomes the penalty for my sin when I avail myself of it. And in his death I find my forgiveness. God in response to my faith applies the merit of Christ's blood to me. That application constitutes my forgiveness.

And so says the Word: "If we confess our sins, he is faithful and just and will forgive us our sins" (1 John 1:9). The entire epistle is declaring the nature of the relation of the blood to its personally available and applied benefits—and that relation is conditional and moral throughout. Here, in this verse, there is no tension between Christ's finished work on the Cross and personally received forgiveness, received on personally met moral terms. God *will* forgive my sins confessed now, even though full provision for that forgiveness, justifying the words "faithful" and "just," was made at Calvary. But the sins were not forgiven then; the forgiveness was *provided* then. They are not and will not be forgiven unless and until I confess them—obviously with true sorrow and all intention of turning from them.

The important accent in Paul's exposition of the gospel is that the death of Christ was made necessary by sin, and was given as an express answer to the demerit of sin—a *hilasterion*, or atonement. While God's own integrity was at issue ("so as to be just," Rom. 3:26), the possibility of extending mercy turned not just on the shed blood, but on the sinner's response, "through faith in his blood" (v. 25).[9] The components are sin—penalty—faith—expiation, not to some mythical public, but to the desperate need of the private sinner. Paul sees the Atonement as thoroughly propitiatory with expiation of the private sinner flowing conditionally. Here is a merging of paid penalty and true forgiveness.

---

[9] To object to this on the ground that to introduce any contingency in the effectiveness of the Atonement is to detract from its sufficiency and make man his own "co-savior," is a desperate kind of illogic. We are only declaring what is plainly written. Furthermore, we are acknowledging a system of personal salvation which is moral, rather than mechanical and pre-programmed.

9

Partakers of God's Integrity

In 1989 a remarkable book was published by Harper & Row, titled *Box 66, Sumac Lane,* written by Edna Hong. Its format is a lengthy correspondence between an author and a publisher, with valuable input (on the side) by the publisher's private secretary. The author has submitted a book on sanctification and the publisher has promptly returned it, with undisguised disdain. Such a subject is outdated, no longer of relevance or interest to the contemporary church. She fires a letter back, with considerable wit and heat, shaming him for such a lame stand, in view of the unmistakable fact that sanctification is a doctrine of the church and is taught in the Bible. Gradually through the give and take of probing and searching letters they both come to a better understanding of what sanctification really is, and how desperately it is needed in the church, after all.[1]

---

[1] A "better understanding" in the mind of the author. While some fine insights were exchanged respecting death to self and the work of the Spirit, the final consensus was on the side of gradualism only. We are sanctified and at the same time we are being sanctified. Properly defined, this is true. But as Paul Rees once said in a hostile setting, "Of course sanctification is a process; but it has to be a crisis before it can be a process."

While this book is unique—weaving enough romance in the heavy theological discussion, that in the end the author and publisher get married!—it is a token of the new awareness in the church these days that *somebody* had better do some deep thinking and clear talking about this matter of sanctification. The lack of it has virtually paralyzed the church and destroyed its moral authority in society.

It is surely appropriate therefore that this book not be completed without showing how the Atonement is a power for holiness. Indeed, omitting it would be very inappropriate.

The Experiential Need

In chapter three it was pointed out that a full salvation required a separation of the sinner from his sin. But this implies far more than pardon. Forgiveness cancels sins of the past, and frees us from their condemnation. As marvelous as this is, it is not in essence a separating of the sinner from his sin. That consists of purifying the sinner from the sin itself, as a clinging pollution. The sinner is not separated from his sin until every known sin is put away, every evil bent broken, and every evil desire purged. This means deliverance from sinful pride, unbelief, self-willfulness, and every unholy affection; in short, being made holy. The standards of holy living need to be so thoroughly internalized that the holy living flows naturally out of the inner person—just as naturally as sinful living flowed previously out of the evil heart (Mark 7:21). The promises of a pure heart can imply nothing less than this (Matt. 5:8; Acts 15:8-9; 1 Tim. 1:5; 2 Tim. 2:22; 1 Pet. 1:22). This is what John Wesley called Christian Perfection.[2]

---

[2]For a balanced perspective on Wesley's teaching, his entire *Plain Account of Christian Perfection* should be read.

The Theological Hurdle

This book has sought to establish the "penal satisfaction" nature of the Atonement. On this foundation rests our justification. By paying the penalty for our sins, Christ reconciled God to us and opened the door for us to become reconciled to God.

But how does this relate to sanctification? Justification is a change in legal standing; sanctification is a change in state. The logical connection between a substitutionary atonement and our personal acquittal is clear enough. But how can atoning blood change our nature? It can set me free from condemnation, but can it change my heart?

The problem is very real, because morally and substantively, justification and sanctification are two different kinds of things. Justification is like the restoration of a stolen car to its proper owner. Sanctification is like the restoration of the car to its proper condition. These acts require completely different agencies. Restoration to the proper owner is juridical, involving—in the case of a stolen car—the police, state agencies, and possibly even courts. But the restoration to a proper condition is accomplished by a different set of people—mechanics and artisans. It is a "hands-on" operation. So likewise our justification is provided for by the blood shed at Calvary; but sanctification is a "hands-on" project. Not just our relation to God needs to be changed, but our likeness to God needs to be restored.

The difference is also illustrated by the hypothetical case of a man condemned to die for a crime committed, but also dying with cancer. He is under a double sentence of death: for what he has done and for what he has. In the one case is a broken law; in the other case an internal disease. The sentence of death as a criminal could conceivably be lifted by a substitute dying in his place. But what would that have to do with his cancer? The problem then is simply, how can a juridical solution to a juridical situation have any bearing on the man's physical condition? What he needs is not only a "penal satisfaction" but a physician.

Perhaps therein we have our answer. What if the substitute were also a physician, and came back from the dead to heal the man? And did not Jesus say, "It is not the healthy who need a doctor, but the sick" (Matt. 9:12)? And did he not assure Saul on the road to Damascus that faith in him would make available not only forgiveness of sins but "a place among those who are sanctified" (Acts 26:18)?

The Biblical Linkage

But before probing more deeply we need to establish the biblical datum of the clear linkage of our sanctification with the cross. The Bible unmistakably identifies sanctification as one of the benefits of Christ's death. This fact will be apparent if we simply highlight some basic passages.

> *For them I sanctify myself, that they too may be truly sanctified* (John 17:19).

> *Christ loved the church and gave himself up for her to make her holy* (Eph. 5:25).

> *Jesus Christ, who gave himself for us to redeem us from all wickedness and to purify for himself a*

people of his very own, eager to do what is good
(Titus 2:14).

And so Jesus also suffered outside the city gate to
make the people holy through his own blood
(Heb.13:12).

Every student well-versed in the Bible knows that the New
Testament is teeming with declarations of the power for holiness which streams from the cross. These verses are only
some of the more direct and obvious.

These passages help us to see that as Christ died for the
world, to bring men and women to God, he also died for the
church. Sanctification, while begun in regeneration, is a blessing for God's people. Sinners must become justified before
they are in the relation to the cross which makes them eligi-
ble for its sanctifying power. When Jesus prayed for the sanctification of his disciples, his petition was preceded by his
declaration, "I am not praying for the world, but for those you
have given me" (John 17:9). And he extended the subjects of
his prayer to include "those who will believe in me through
their message"(v. 20). Christ is praying for the sanctification
of every believer, in every age—a possibility which he links to
his own death as its means: "For them I sanctify myself"—set
myself apart in death—"that they too may be truly sanctified."[3]

---

[3]The three instances of *hagiazo* in John 17:17-19 are aorist
imperative, present indicative, and perfect passive, in that order. There
is here a bold petition of the Son to the Father for a definite work to
be done. The work is to be grounded in Christ's self-sanctification for

It is significant, also, that in every case these passages verbally are governed by the subjunctive mode, meaning not absolute certainty but possibility. Jesus died *in order* that his disciples might be truly sanctified, *in order* that he might sanctify (NASB) the church, *in order* that he might purify his people, and *in order* that the worshipers might be made holy.

This possibility is double-edged. One edge warns us that in spite of Christ's purpose in his death for our sanctification, we may miss it—just as we may miss justification in spite of the adequacy of the provision. The death of Christ did not actually or automatically accomplish the entire sanctification of his disciples, or the sanctification of the church, or the purification of his people, or the sanctification of the worshipers. Rather his death made this sanctification possible.

The other edge is the reminder that the very possibility of becoming holy is totally dependent on Christ's atoning death. If there had been no cross there could be no holiness, either in this life or in the next. It was as necessary for Christ to die to make us holy as it was for him to die to make us free. We cannot be justified by his blood then proceed to achieve our own sanctification. In the words of Cecil F. Alexander,

> *He died that we might be forgiv'n,*
> *He died to make us good,*
> *That we might go at last to heav'n,*
> *Saved by His precious blood.*

---

the cross. The declared objective is that they may come into a fullness of true sanctification as a state or condition, the product of a work of grace.

Full salvation, then, includes both justification and sanctification, and both are boons of the Atonement.

The Dynamic of the Spirit

But we are right back to our original problem. Blood can *atone* for sin, but how can blood reach my heart, and make a subjective change in me?

We must pick up the thread of an earlier hint. Our Substitute is also our Physician, who rose from the dead to implement by his Spirit all the direct and *indirect* benefits of the Atonement. In the act of atoning for our sins Christ cleared the way for the sanctifying ministry of the Spirit. Another way to put it is to say that he provided a moral footing in a new relationship with God for the inward workings of his grace to begin to be accomplished.

It is the Holy Spirit who convicts of sin and draws us to a crucified, resurrected Christ as the answer to our sin. It is he who regenerates us, and in so doing creates not just spiritual life within us but a kind of spiritual life which is holy, with holy impulses and affinities. It is he who gives to the believer a new moral power to sluff off the old life and put on the new. In this radical change is the beginning of a very real sanctification (cf. 1 Cor. 6:9-11). It is this same Spirit who probes, searches, illumines, draws, and disciplines until he succeeds in crowding us back to the cross for the second touch, and in a total surrender let this Christ-Spirit baptize us into his fullness (cf. 2 Thess. 2:13; 1 Pet. 1:2). In all of this the "in order that" of the cross is being worked out in the heart of the believer, and the "power of the blood" proved to be powerful indeed.

Theologically, we may say then that pardon is purchased by the blood, while holiness is mediated by the blood.[4] William Greathouse interprets Wesley as teaching that "on the basis of the Atonement and through the agency of the Spirit, every penitent sinner may be saved 'from the guilt and power of sin,' and every justified believer may be purified in heart and enabled to live a life of sanctity and Christlike servanthood."[5]

God's Wisdom

Let us now assemble some of the ways the apostle Paul sees more in the cross than justification. His classic summary of the total salvation package in Christ is 1 Corinthians 1:30: "It is because of him that you are in Christ Jesus, who has become for us wisdom from God—that is, our righteousness, holiness, and redemption." The connection with the cross is in vv. 23-24: "But we preach Christ crucified: a stumbling block to Jews and foolishness to Gentiles, but to those whom God has called, Christ the power of God and the wisdom of God." The cross does two things: release moral power and display God's wisdom. The wisdom of humanism rises no high-

---

[4]This is why 1 John 1:7—"But if we walk in the light...the blood of Jesus, his Son, purifies us from all sin"—was not listed above. Bible students are not agreed as to whether this is the purification of expiation, ascribable directly to the blood, or the purification of sanctification ascribable indirectly to the blood. When the blood is said to cleanse, expiation is more likely the intent. In the Hebrews passage the sanctifying of the people is "through" his blood, dia with the genitive, indicating an ultimate accomplishment. See Chamberlain's Exegetical Greek Grammar of the New Testament, p. 117.

[5]Nazarene Theological Seminary *Tower* (Fall, 1988), p. 7. Extract from commencement address.

er than self-effort based on ignorance of the real state of affairs. This then is not wisdom but stupidity. In contrast, God sees the stark reality of man's degradation and bondage, and in divine wisdom has appointed the crucifixion of his Son as the means of extricating man from his utterly helpless predicament.

The deliverance has three facets: justification, sanctification, and glorification. God through Christ's atoning work has made these three blessings available to all who are in Christ by faith. In Christ we are delivered from our past and set into a new relationship to God. In Christ we are delivered from our depravity and brought into a new state of holiness. In Christ we are assured of the ultimate redemption from this earthly environment, with its physical disease and moral hazards. In that ultimate triumph our redemption will be consummated. The cross therefore purchased for us full salvation from sin in this life and resurrection into glorified bodies in the next. Marvelous divine wisdom! Only an Infinite Mind could devise and implement such a plan.

Our Crucifixion with Christ

This trilogy of blessings provides the basic framework of Paul's exposition of the gospel in Romans 1-8. The Atonement proper, i.e., its propitiatory nature as the basis for justification, is the focus of Romans 1-5 (some would say 1-4). Sanctification is the focus of Romans 6-8 (or 5-8).[6] Romans

---

[6]Some would put the break between justification and sanctification at 6:1. J. Kenneth Grider, however, in his *A Wesleyan Holiness Theology,* makes a strong case for 5:2, based in part on the NASB rendering.

8 also points to our ultimate redemption, or glorification, in the future.

The new note introduced in these chapters is that our sanctification was provided at the cross as well as our justification. In unfolding this, Paul introduces a new preposition. He has been speaking of Christ dying "for" our sins (Rom. 4:25; 5:6, 8); now he speaks of Christ dying "to" sin—and of our dying with him.

This transition is prompted by Paul's anticipation of a misunderstanding of grace—exactly the same misunderstanding that plagues the church today. In affirming Christ's atoning death as the only ground of our justification, Paul has established the truth that our salvation is all of grace, not at all of works. But he was shrewd enough to know that some would promptly read into this a perception of grace as being permissive toward sin. So he faces this cute little twist head-on, and indignantly repudiates it. "Shall we go on sinning so that grace may increase? By no means! We died to sin; how can we live in it any longer?" (Rom. 6:1-2).

There is the new preposition—died *to* sin. This is the implication of our union with Christ, a union not only with Christ in his life but first of all in his death. "The death he died, he died to sin once for all; but the life he lives, he lives to God" (v. 10). Now comes the punch line: "In the same way, count yourselves dead to sin but alive to God in Christ Jesus" (v. 11).

To be dead to sin is to be unresponsive to its appeal and delivered from its power. This is a difficult concept when applied to Christ, for he was never alive to sin. But his death was nevertheless a death to sin in the sense that all conflict with the satanic forces of evil was ended. He was now beyond the reach of temptation or of satanic wiles. While our identification with him does not put an end in this life to the reach of temptation or the wiles of the devil, it is nevertheless a breaking of sin's deadlock on us, so that we are free now to be fully alive to God.

And Paul grounds this new power for holiness squarely in the dying of Christ. "For we know that our old self was crucified with him so that the body of sin might be done away with, that we should no longer be slaves to sin—because anyone who has died has been freed from sin."[7] To refer this to our physical death, which for all who read these lines is yet future, would be a colossal blunder. What Paul is saying is that just as our sins, plural, were nailed to the cross, so also our sinful nature finds its remedy in the cross. Jesus died for our sin as well as our sins. The old nature was crucified with Jesus in order that our personal "body of sin" might be put to death.

The term "body of sin" finds its definition in Romans 7, where Paul discusses the problem underlying *sins*, plural. He says it is the *dwelling-in-me-sin*, or the sinful nature with which we come into the world, which prompts repeated sinning in spite of resolutions to the contrary. When he exclaims "Who will rescue me from this body of death?" he is referring to the innate problem which he has just been describing. He is not asking for someone to put him to death physically that he might escape this earthly body. Paul was not a Gnostic who

---

[7]"Our old man," says C. K. Barrett, is "Adam—or rather ourselves in union with Adam." *The Epistle to the Romans* (New York: Harper & Brothers, 1957), p. 125.

thought the body was essentially evil and needed to be escaped as soon as possible, that the soul might be pure. On the contrary Paul is viewing the sin principle within as a unitary nature, in this sense a "body."

The answer is exultant: "Thanks be to God—through Jesus Christ our Lord!" (Rom. 7:24-25). But this is recapitulation. He had already declared that this nature was crucified with Christ, meaning that the solution to our inner sin problem was the objective of the Atonement as well as the solution to our guilt problem—"so that the body of sin might be done away with."

The precise nature of this deliverance is delineated in Romans 8. He has just said that the answer to his question, "Who shall deliver…?" is "through Jesus Christ." Now he enlarges on this answer: "through Christ Jesus the law of the Spirit of life set me free from the law of sin and death." Now Paul is confirming the earlier insight, namely, that while the Atonement included sanctification in its provision, the implementation of this provision is accomplished personally and individually by the Spirit. Calvary—provision; Pentecost—experience.

And it is a real "setting free." That which blocked the effectiveness of the Law—this inner sin principle—was condemned by Christ as our "sin offering." Thus Christ's death not only absorbed the condemnation for our sins, but constituted a judgment or condemnation against the sin nature. There is provision for that too. It is condemned in such a way that not only is its hold broken but its presence purged. This results in a totally new moral power, "that the righteous requirements of the law might be fully met in us, who do not live according to the sinful nature but according to the Spirit" (Rom. 8:4).

The New Covenant

It is becoming clear, therefore, that while the "penal satisfaction" nature of the Atonement is the basis for our justification, this does not exhaust the meaning of the Atonement. But it clears the way for the establishment of the new covenant with and in the believer, in its full richness. When Jesus said "This is the blood of the covenant, which is poured out for many for the forgiveness of sins,"[8] He was not implying that the forgiveness of sins was the whole of the covenant. Elsewhere we learn that it is exactly what Ezekiel foretold: "I will give you a new heart and put a new spirit in you; I will remove from you your heart of stone and give you a heart of flesh. And I will put my Spirit in you and move you to follow my decrees and be careful to keep my laws" (Ezek. 36:26-27). This is not a prediction of an intensified legalism but of new moral power springing from a transformed nature.

Jeremiah writes of the "new covenant" in similar terms.

> I will put my law in their minds
> and write it on their hearts.
> I will be their God,
> and they will be my people (31:33).

That this finds its perfect fulfillment in and through Christ is made clear by the writer to the Hebrews in chapters 8 and

---

[8]Some manuscripts add "new" which, of course, is implied. See Luke 22:20 and 1 Corinthians 11:25 where the word is used.

10. Therefore Christ's blood was not only the means of expiating personal sin but the ratification of the new covenant with his justified people. But whereas the ratifying blood for the Sinaitic covenant was powerless to change the people, our Lord's blood had in it the release of the sanctifying Spirit.

When by faith we are justified, we are brought into a living relationship with God. It is a relationship of peace: "Therefore, since we have been justified through faith, we have peace with God" (Rom. 5:1). It is also a relationship of "access by faith into this grace in which we now stand" (v. 2). Furthermore we "rejoice in the hope of the glory of God" and are enabled to "rejoice in our sufferings" through God's love which has been poured "into our hearts by the Holy Spirit, whom he has given us" (vv. 2-5).

Paul reaches a climactic summary in the words, "Not only is this so, but we also rejoice in God through our Lord Jesus Christ, through whom we have now received reconciliation" (v. 11). Rejoice in God! Only the inward experience of the new covenant in its full richness can enable us to rejoice in God. Without this *fullness* we may believe in God, fear him, be thankful to him, serve him, and seek to obey him, but we do not *rejoice* in him. We may rejoice in his blessings, but not *in him*. This speaks of an intimate relationship of unshadowed communion. This is indeed what may properly be called "perfect love," the kind that casts out fear (1 John 4:18). This is the end product of the Atonement when it is allowed to do its full work. And this is sanctification.

Our joy in God is weak, fearful, and intermittent, as long as we are yet carnal (in the Corinthian sense, 1 Cor. 3:1-4). Any remaining reluctance to embrace Christ's full lordship in our lives, any deep controversy still in progress between us and God, any unchristlike spirit of unforgiveness or self-seeking which still tarnishes our devotion, impairs the openness and freedom of perfect communion with God. To this degree our sanctification is yet partial. That this falls short of our privilege is implied by Paul's wish-prayer for the Thessalonians: "Now may the God of peace Himself sanctify you entirely, and may your spirit and soul and body be preserved complete, without blame at the coming of our Lord Jesus Christ" (1 Thess. 5:23, NASB).

This dynamic power for holiness which streams from the cross is what H. Orton Wiley calls the "vital principle" of the Atonement.[9] The Atonement makes possible the redemptive indwelling of persons by the Spirit, who not only alters their direction but their core-affinities. In the psychological sense the "moral influence" of the Atonement now shows its power, for when penitent sinners find their new life in Christ, the very intensity of their relief and gratitude generates a love which desires to please Christ. But the psychological effect cannot carry the whole load—there is the direct action of the Holy Spirit in strengthening these new desires and resolves, and imparting the inward enablement (Phil. 2:5-13). In fact, when obeyed he will stop at nothing less than the complete crucifixion of the carnal mind.

A definite stage in this process is obedience to Romans

---

[9]*Christian Theology*, vol. II, p. 276ff.

12:1-2. The Spirit urges upon us the duty, out of love and gratitude, to make a decisive presentation of all our "ransomed powers" as a burnt offering—but one which while kept on the altar in one sense is all over the place in another, not *passively* surrendered to God's will, but *actively and eagerly* concentrating the whole of life in all its facets to the glory and service of God.

This total devotion finds its expression also in the crucifixion motif. Paul has explained how we were crucified with Christ, and that that identification may become personal and experiential, not only in the knowledge of sins nailed to the cross but in the knowledge that self is crucified with Christ. What is historical fact needs also to be personal fact, which can enable us to share with Paul the testimony, "I have been crucified with Christ and I no longer live, but Christ lives in me. The life I live in the body, I live by faith in the Son of God, who loved me and gave himself for me" (Gal. 2:20). The cross inspires this devotion, the Spirit internalizes it. When this is actually one's experience he can also say with Paul, "May I never boast except in the cross of our Lord Jesus Christ, through which the world has been crucified to me, and I to the world" (Gal. 6:14).

It is this identification and internalization which enables the believer to literally live by the cross-principle. When the cross governs the whole of life, then money, talents, time, associations, ambitions, goals, reputation, are all laid under tribute to the one passion, to please God in Christ, not grudgingly but joyfully.

Redemption

When Jesus said that he came to give his life a "ransom for many" (*lutron*, Matt. 20:28; cf. Mark 10:45), and Paul later echoed his Lord's statement in even stronger terms, "gave himself as a ransom [*antilutron*] for all men" (1 Tim. 2:6), we are given an insight into a central meaning of the cross, one that provides a further clue to the way in which the Atonement effects our sanctification.

The redemption motif is seen in the Exodus, when the blood of a lamb secured a family from the slaying of the firstborn. God used this to assert his claim over the nation, as having been redeemed out of Egyptian slavery. The Passover feast therefore was a reminder both of deliverance and of divine ownership.

These two meanings were intrinsic to Christ's payment of ransom. Paul reminds the Corinthians, "You are not your own; you were bought at a price" (1 Cor. 6:19-20). More than this, our body is a temple of the Holy Spirit. God's property and God's temple, "Therefore honor God with your body." Our ransom places us under obligation to live holy lives, remembering to whom we belong. This is our conscious and chosen response.

But the deliverance side of the action underlies the truth of ownership. Christ gave his life a ransom for us in the sense that he redeemed us from bondage. He set us free. We could say that the release from condemnation in justification constitutes the purchased freedom. But bondage is more than the imposed burden of guilt, it is also helplessness and servitude. It is Romans 7. It is slavery to the "empty way of life handed down to you from your forefathers"; from this you were "redeemed" (1 Pet. 1:18). Redemption therefore is more than purchase, it is emancipation from two kinds of slavery: slavery to sin and legalistic bondage to the Mosaic Law.

The natural man's threefold bondage is to the world, the flesh, and the devil. Grace delivers us from the iron grip of the world and from the pollution of the flesh partly through the conquest of Satan. There is a mysterious connection here, but it is germane to the whole question of the power of the cross for sanctification. Satan had not only a real claim to this planet but access to every human heart to a tyrannical degree. The Son invaded his territory, became a man as exposed to Satan as others, fought him to a standstill in the wilderness, then destroyed his claim on the human race at Calvary. Jesus "shared in their humanity, so that by his death he might destroy him who holds the power of death—that is, the devil—and free those who were held in slavery all their lives by their fear of death" (Heb. 2:14-15). Jesus, by vanquishing Satan put chains on his depradations, especially in respect to believers.

Satan and his evil cohorts thought they had won by making a public spectacle of Jesus, but it was the other way around: "And having disarmed the powers and authorities, he made a public spectacle of them, triumphing over them by the cross" (Col.2:15).

All of this introduces the Ransom theory of the Atonement, which Gustaf Aulen in his *Christus Victor* claims to be the classic view, holding virtual sway until Anselm. A ransom is a price paid for the release of hostages. The age-old question has been, To whom was the price paid? The primitive answer was, to the devil. A more theologically mature and sophisticated church says the price was paid to God—in other words, the satisfaction theory.

But it has already been seen that this is not to be interpreted crassly, as if God were a hostage-holder. The need for a price was inherent in the total morality of the situation, including the nature of sin and the holiness of God. We have gone over that ground. And Satan was certainly an important force in the drama of redemption, both in bringing about man's sinful condition and in holding sway over the world; therefore Christ's death needed to serve the purpose not only of providing a penal satisfaction for man's sin but of breaking the power of Satan. Whether Satan fully understood the dynamics of what God was doing is doubtful; otherwise he would have tried to prevent the crucifixion instead of plotting it. At any rate he overstepped himself, as did the Witch in Narnia when she killed Aslan, and in the process brought about her own decisive and final defeat.

C. Anderson Scott says that "'Christ pronounced the doom of sin.' Sin was henceforth deposed from its autocratic power."[10] But by personifying sin in this way, Scott is implying a personal Adversary in the background who is responsible for the pervasiveness of sin and, through his activities, augments

---

[10] "Romans," *The Abingdon Bible Commentary* (New York: The Abingdon Press, 1929), p. 1153. Quoted by William H. Greathouse in an unpublished essay, "Christus Victor," in which he seeks to show that this motif provides the strongest ground for a doctrine of entire sanctification.

sin's tyrannical power. Christ delivers us from sin not only because he has paid our penalty, but because he has dissolved the power of Satan. "The sinner is under the bondage of Satan and sin; Christ's redemptive act delivers man from bondage and sets him at liberty," says Greathouse. Also he writes:

> Christ's victory for us in the Atonement becomes Christ's victory in us by the indwelling Spirit (Rom. 8:1-11). Christ's victory is reproduced in us. In the Holy Spirit Christ for us becomes Christ in us, recapitulating in our history His triumph over sin. This is the meaning of Christus Victor for sanctification.[11]

The precise relevance of this to sanctification is brought into still sharper focus by Greathouse in linking 1 John 3:8 with 1 John 3:4. In the first passage we are told that Jesus came to "destroy the devil's work," while in the second we read that "sin is lawlessness." Greathouse comments: "John means Christ came to destroy the principle of lawlessness (*anomia*...), which was the devil's chief work in man."[12]

The stress therefore on Christ's death as a ransom is on its power to release us from the threefold bondage. Satan is bound, even now, and though he may temporarily rage and roar as the "accuser of our brothers," they overcome "him by the blood of the Lamb and by the word of their testimony" (Rev. 12:10b-11). His power to tempt, deceive, and harass is

---

[11]Greathouse, "Christus Victor," p. 4.
[12]Ibid., p. 6.

chained. The moral power of Satan's defeat is available to us through grace, so that "we should no longer be slaves to sin" (Rom. 6:6).

And as far as the world is concerned, Jesus said, "In the world you will have trouble. But take heart! I have overcome the world" (John 16:33). Because he overcame the world, we may overcome the world. The secret, according to John, is our faith: "This is the victory that has overcome the world, even our faith" (1 John 5:4b). This is not the faith of a pollyanna optimism, but a very specific faith: "Who is it that overcomes the world? Only he who believes that Jesus is the Son of God" (v. 5). The Spirit not only assures us of the truth of who *Jesus* is, but assures us of the truth of who *we* are:

> We know also that we are children of God, and that the whole world is under the control of the evil one. We know also that the Son of God has come and has given us understanding, so that we may know him that is true. And we are in him that is true—even in his Son Jesus Christ. He is the true God and eternal life (vv. 19-20).

When we know who Christ is, and who we are in him, we see the falseness of the world, and its spell on us is broken forever. When we grasp the truth with spiritual eyes wide open, we will never again be taken in by the world's sham. No matter how glamorous or promising the world may seem to be, it holds no appeal for the one who has seen Christ in his matchless beauty, and caught a glimpse of eternal realities. The world's values are no longer ours, and so we no longer feel the need to chase after its baubles.

Victory indeed!—over the flesh, the world, and the devil! This is the heritage of those who by faith have entered into the full measure of their privileges in Christ: their entire sanctification.

"He who calls you is faithful, who also will do it" (1 Thess. 5:24, NKJV) When will God do it? When in full conformity to his terms we ask him! Let us ask, even now.

Bibliography

Aulen, Gustaf. *Christus Victor*. Trans. by A.G. Herbert. New York: The MacMillan Co., 1961. Historical survey. Stress on the Cross as victory over Satan, sin, and death.

Byrum, Russell R. *Christian Theology*. Revision editor, Arlo F. Newell. Anderson, IN: Warner Press, 1982. In treating the Atonement, Byrum takes a mediating Arminian position; preserves the propitiatory note.

Collins, Kenneth J. *The Scripture Way of Salvation: The Heart of John Wesley's Theology*. Nashville: Abingdon Press, 1997. Perhaps the best treatment of Wesley's doctrine available.

Denney, James. *The Death of Christ. Its Place and Interpretation in the New Testament*. New York: Hodder & Stoughton, n.d. Powerfully defends the basic note of propitiation.

Dunning, H. Ray. *Grace, Faith, and Holiness*. Kansas City, MO: Beacon Hill Press, 1988. A systematic theology. Argues that a doctrine of Atonement should be consonant with its benefits: prevenient grace, reconciliation, including justification, and sanctification.

Gould, J. Glenn. *The Precious Blood of Christ*. Kansas City, MO: Beacon Hill Press, 1959. A classic introductory survey for the beginner.

Grider, J. Kenneth. *A Wesleyan-Holiness Theology*. Kansas City, MO: Beacon Hill Press, 1994. A systematic theology. Clear delineation of the various theories of the Atonement; espouses the Governmental theory, but concedes that the Atonement's necessity is grounded both in the requirements of moral government and the divine nature.

Miley, John. *The Atonement in Christ*. New York: Hunt & Eaton, 1879. The classic Methodist exposition of the Governmental theory.

Oden, Thomas C. *The Word of Life*. Systematic Theology, Vol. Two, pp. 279-501. San Francisco: HarperSanFrancisco. A highly readable, thoroughly Wesleyan compendium of the doctrine of Atonement based directly on Scripture and drawing from the teachings of the Church Fathers.

Purkiser, W. T., Richard S. Taylor, Willard H. Taylor. *God, Man, and Salvation*. Kansas City, MO: Beacon Hill Press, 1977. A biblical theology. Chapters relating to the Atonement are written by Willard Taylor, who sees the cross as both a judgment upon sin and a vicarious or substitutionary act on the part of Christ.

Shelton, R. Larry. "Initial Salvation: The Redemptive Grace of God in Christ," *A Contemporary Wesleyan Theology*. Charles W. Carter, editor. Grand Rapids, MI: Francis Asbury Press (Zondervan), 1983. A very comprehensive, concise and balanced treatment. Keeps objective and subjective aspects, also expiation vs. propitiation, representative and substitutional motifs, in balance.

Stott, John R. W. *The Cross of Christ*. Downers Grove, IL: InterVarsity Press, 1986. A contemporary classic in the Reformed tradition. While far from antinomian, Stott falls short of seeing in the Atonement provision for that degree of sanctification which Wesleyans believe to be the heart and core of salvation available now.

Summers, Thomas O. *Systematic Theology*. Ed. & annotated by T.R. Tigert. Nashville: House of Methodist Episcopal Church South, 1902. Profound treatment. Excellent exposition and critique of various theories. Perhaps the most cogent refutation of John Miley available.

Swinburne, Richard. *Responsibility and Atonement*. Oxford: Clarendon Press, 1989. Psychological and moral philosophy approach. The Cross was provided by God as a means of satisfying man's need for reparation, not as a means of satisfying the divine holiness.

Taylor, Vincent. *Forgiveness and Reconciliation*. London: MacMillan and Co., Limited, 1952. Second edition. Concedes the penal element in the Atonement but denies its necessity as the ground of forgiveness.

Trevethan, Thomas L. *The Beauty of God's Holiness*. Downers Grove, IL: InterVarsity Press, 1995. Relates the Atonement to God's awesome and uncompromising holiness.

Wilcox, Leslie D., editor. *Profiles in Wesleyan Theology*, Volume Two. Salem, OH: Schmul Publishing Co., Inc., 1984. Readings with commentary on the doctrine of Atonement and related issues, from Bishop E.B. Kephart, John Miley, William Burt Pope, Olin Curtis, Daniel Steele, A.M. Hills, and Bishop R.S. Foster.

Wiley, H. Orton. *Christian Theology*. Volume Two. Kansas City, MO: Nazarene Publishing House, 1941. Chapters XXIII and XXIV are foundational studies. Opposes the Calvinistic form of the Penal Satisfaction theory, but maintains that propitiation is the deepest note in the doctrine of Atonement.

Wiley, H. Orton. *The Epistle to the Hebrews.* Kansas City, MO: Beacon Hill Press, 1959. Edited and revised by Morris A. Weigelt, 1984.

Other Studies

Barnes, Albert. *On the Atonement.* Minneapolis: Bethany Press, 1980.

Berkhof, Louis. *Vicarious Atonement Through Christ.* Grand Rapids: Wm. B. Eerdmans Publishing Company, 1936.

Bruce, Alexander B. *The Humiliation of Christ.* Grand Rapids: Wm. W. Eerdmans Publishing Company, 1955.

Cave, Sydney. *The Doctrine of the Work of Christ.* Nashville: Cokesbury Press, 1937.

Coppedge, Allan. *John Wesley in Theological Debate.* Wilmore, KY: Wesley Heritage Press, 1987.

Dale, R.W. *The Atonement.* London: Congregational Union of England and Wales, 1900.

Forsyth, P. T. *Positive Preaching and Modern Mind.* New York: George H. Doran Company, n.d.

Gamertsfelder, S.J. *Systematic Theology.* Harrisburg, PA: Evangelical Publishing House, 1921.

Haldeman, I.M. *The Tabernacle, Priesthood, and Offerings.* Westwood, N.J.: Fleming H. Revell Company, 1925.

Hartley, John E. and R. Larry Shelton, editors. *An Inquiry into Biblical Soteriology.* Wesleyan Theological Perspectives, Vol. 1. Anderson, IN: Warner Press, 1981.

Henry, Carl F.H., editor. *Basic Christian Doctrines.* Cf. Chapters 22-24. Grand Rapids: Baker Book House, 1962.

Hills, A.M. *Fundamental Christian Theology*. Two vols. Pasadena, CA: C.J. Kinne, publisher, 1931. Cf. Vol. II, Part V.

Lewis, C. S. "The Humanitarian Theory of Punishment," *God in the Dock*. Grand Rapids, MI: William B. Eerdmans, 1970.

McGrath, Alister E., editor. *The Blackwell Encyclopedia of Modern Christian Thought*. Cambridge, MA: Blackwell Publishers, Inc., 1993. "Soteriology," pp. 616-626, by the editor.

McGrath, Alister E. *The Mystery of the Cross*. Grand Rapids: Zondervan Publishing house, 1988.

McKim, Donald K., editor. *A Guide to Contemporary Hermeneutics*. Grand Rapids, MI: William B. Eerdmans, 1986.

Merrill, Stephen M. *The Atonement: A Brief Study*. Cincinnati: Jennings & Pye, 1901.

Morris, Leon. *The Atonement. Its Meaning and Significance*. Downers Grove, IL: InterVarsity Press, 1983.

Morris, Leon. *The Cross in the New Testament*. William B. Eerdmans, 1965.

Packer, J. I. "What Did the Cross Achieve? The Logic of Penal Substitution," *Tyndale Bulletin*, 25 (1974), pp. 3-45.

Pinkham, William P. *The Lamb of God: or, The Scriptural Philosophy of the Atonement*. Edited by Anna L. Spann. Portland, OR: Evangel Publishers, 1946.

Shank, Robert. *Life in the Son: A Study in the Doctrine of Perseverance*. Springfield, MO: Westcott Publishers, 1964.

Stibbs, Alan. *The Meaning of the Word "Blood" in Scripture.* London: The Tyndale Press, 1948.

Taylor, Richard S. *The Scandal of Pre-forgiveness.* Salem, OH: Schmul Publishing Co., 1993.

Taylor, Richard S. *A Right Conception of Sin.* Kansas City, MO: Beacon Hill Press, 1939.

Taylor, Richard S. The Theological Formulation, Vol. III, *Exploring Christian Holiness.* Kansas City, MO: Beacon Hill Press of Kansas City, 1985.

Townsend, L.T. *God's Goodness and Severity.* Cincinnati: Jennings & Pye, 1902.

Yocum, Dale. *Creeds in Contrast.* Salem, OH: Schmul Publishing Co., Inc., 1986.

Index